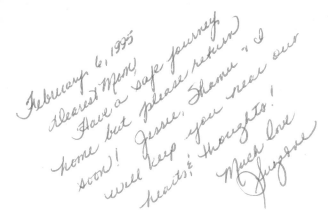

*February 6, 1995*
*Dearest Mom,*
*Have a safe journey*
*home but please return*
*soon! Jessie, Shannon & I*
*will keep you near our*
*hearts & thoughts!*
*Much love*
*Suzanne*

# THE TIMES TRAVEL LIBRARY

Edited by Paul Zach and Gretchen Liu

Times Editions, 1 New Industrial Road, Singapore 1953
© 1987 Times Editions Pte Ltd
Reprinted 1992

Printed by Kyodo Printing Co (S) Pte Ltd, Singapore
Color separation by Columbia, Singapore
Typeset by Superskill Graphics, Singapore

**Cover:** Every night, spotlights illuminate the National
Monument (Monas) in Independence Square, the heart
of Jakarta's government district. The 137-meter tall
white obelisk, topped by a bronze flame painted with
32 kilograms of gold leaf, is the most conspicuous
symbol of the young nation's strength and virility.
**Endpapers:** Another striking physical characteristic of
the capital is its tightly-packed clusters of low-rise
residences, most with roofs of red slate. From the air,
the rooftops seem to stretch to the horizon.
**Frontispiece:** Garuda, the heroic eagle of the epic
Ramayana legend, a shield and motto are part of
Indonesia's coat of arms which is a familiar sight
throughout Jakarta. The figures on the shield represent
the state ideology Pancasila or "five principles": the
star signifies belief in one god; the head of the native
*banteng* buffalo stands for the nation's sovereignty; the
banyan tree represents the national consciousness; the
round links of the chain symbolize woman, the square
man — interlinked they stand for democracy; and
social justice is symbolized by the sheaves of the rice
and cotton plants that provide the peoples' basic
necessities — food and clothing. The words *Bhinneka
Tunggal Ika* mean "Unity in Diversity," the national
motto that has united the people of Indonesia's vast
archipelago despite their hundreds of diverse cultures
and languages. Take particular note of Garuda's
feathers: there are eight on the tail, 17 on each wing and
45 on the neck, a subtle reminder of August 17, 1945,
the date of Indonesia's proclamation of independence.

ISBN: 9971-40-044-8

# JAKARTA

*We hope you take good memories of Jakarta with you, and it was great to share the adventure with you.*
*Love Simon and Deb. XX 5/2/95.*

Photographs by

Diane Graham Garth, Emmo Italiaander,
John Paul Kay, R. Ian Lloyd, Leonard Lueras,
Kal Muller and Luca Invernizzi Tettoni

Text by Paul Zach and Mary Jane Edleson

JONAThANBromLe

Designed by Leonard Lueras

*It was wonderful to me you and enjoy some good times and shopping together. Sampai bertemu lagi. A bu prochaine! Safe Journey. Selamat jalan dan sampai jumpa lagi lu. Anthorie Tom*

*Dot have a good trip and come back soon Martin*

*Dot, it was great getting to know you. I'm glad we got to spend time together. We somehow the same time so somehow wish you soon going too. See you I think Nicky watch out for traffic in the states*

TIMES EDITIONS

*This page:* The white-tiled domes of Istiqlal Mosque, Southeast Asia's largest, dominate Central Jakarta.

*Following pages:* Dock workers stroll past a row of traditional Bugis *pinisi* schooners at ancient Sunda Kelapa; a sculpture by prominent Indonesian artist But Mokhtar called "Aesthetical Element" stands at the end of a fountain in front of Jakarta's Parliament Building, Gedung DPR-MPR; lush tropical greenery shades Jakarta's pleasant Menteng district by day; and swirls of light brighten the burgeoning Jalan M.H. Thamrin commercial district at night.

# Contents

*A form of parliamentary democracy* is practiced under the architecturally-striking, winged roofs of Gedung DPR-MPR near the Jakarta Hilton Hotel. Jakarta is the capital of Indonesia, a vast archipelago of more than 13,677 islands. In this building, elected representatives from the most far-flung islands gather to determine the nation's laws and policies.

# Jakarta

## *The Meeting Place*

**M**orning begins early in Jakarta, as it has for centuries. People begin stirring long before the sun splashes color into the dusky grays that cloak the city's vast sea of red slate roof tiles just before the rosy dawn.

"*Allahu Akhbar! Allahu Akhbar!*" The amplified song of *Azan Suboh* trickles into the morning calm. The ripples of sound from a loudspeaker or two rapidly gain momentum as chants from hundreds of mosques join in. Within minutes, a torrent of praying voices engulfs the awakening city.

Some of the people of Jakarta pull pillows over their heads and roll over. Others, insulated from the waves of sound by the hum of their air-conditioners, barely stir.

But many devout Muslims rouse themselves from sleep for the first of the day's five prayer sessions. Whole families shake off slumber. They dump icy water over their heads, scooped from a *bak*, the tiled vat in their bathrooms. Mothers and daughters don the traditional white veil, the *tudong*. Fathers and sons cover their head with the ubiquitous black or white caps, the *peci*. Then they face in the direction of Mecca, kneel on prayer rugs, prostrate themselves and praise God.

Outside, hundreds of others are already drifting into the cool, damp streets. Some stretch, touch their toes and move into a brisk walk. Some jog. On Sundays, city authorities close off parts of the main traffic arteries in the city so that men and women can bring their children, even babies, for an early work-out or simply a refreshing stroll.

On weekdays the business of survival takes precedence. Sunrise finds some people wading in stagnant ponds of water in the Setiabudi area just south of the wealthy Menteng district in search of fish larvae which they net, collect in plastic bags tied to their waists, and later sell as feedstock to ornamental fish dealers. In south Jakarta, peddlers in Pasar Manggarai and Pasar Minggu pump up their kerosene lanterns as hundreds amicably jostle each other for the best pick of *kangkung*, *bayam*, *kacang panjang*, *cabe*, papaya, rambutan, and other fresh vegetables, spices and fruits. Other self-employed retailers load up wooden carts and head off in all directions to sell their produce door-to-door and on streets and sidewalks. A few wiry men race past them through the smooth main streets transporting passengers aboard their *becak* pedicabs before daylight banishes them to back alleys.

Thousands take to the streets to hawk fried rice or cooked-to-order chicken porridge, a

breakfast staple, from their mobile fast-food wagons. Women, wearing the traditional, form-fitting *sarong kebaya*, carry baskets like backpacks from which they hawk bottles of *jamu*, an Indonesian herbal medicine.

"*Minya-a-ak!*" cry the cooking oil peddlers who push their cans through the streets, towels hung from their necks to soak up perspiration. The sun climbs into Jakarta's dewy sky fast and relentlessly. It seems closer, bigger, more intense here, in this land so near the equator. Its heat both stimulates and drains.

The steady procession of peddlers religiously makes its way through the streets of Jakarta every morning. Like the cooking oil pushers,

**Selamat Datang** *is the Indonesian way of saying welcome and Jakarta's famous statue of a waving couple (left) — now swamped by the rapid growth of traffic, hotels and buildings proudly displaying the Indonesian flag and seal (above) — says it all.*

some announce their arrival with a patented shriek. Others bang gongs or knock out wooden rhythms with hollow bamboo sticks.

The ingenuity that goes into the noisemaking of these street people is exceeded only by the amazing spectrum of their occupations. A wizened old man hunches under the weight of a bamboo pole that straddles his shoulders. From either end of the pole dangles a veritable menagerie of tropical fish, birds and other small pets in jars and cages. At bus stops, youngsters approach the queues beginning to build up and proffer shoeshines, even to those wearing sandals or tennis shoes. On Jalan Wahid Hasyim, behind the Sari Pacific Hotel, a constant parade of booksellers cradle stacks of paperbacks in their arms and inevitably turn up when you enter one of the street's many "*Foto*" processing stores. Many shopkeepers roll up their shutters and open by 7 a.m.

The lack of a storefront, however, does not stop the ebullient people of Jakarta from engaging in freewheeling enterprise. The highways ringing Jakarta are lined with stalls that sell everything — including kitchen sinks. Some sell tacky stone or plaster reproductions, for use as lawn and garden ornaments. Doric columns, "Venus de Milo" and the "Winged Victory" stand next to the more appropriate Gaja Madah and Hanuman, characters from Indonesian history and legend. On the next stretch of road, a man sells pup tents. The youths who tend these ubiquitous concerns, cover their mouths with handtowels, like bandits, to shield themselves against the dust and fumes. Other youths ply the streets selling the handtowels. If there is a hundred rupiah to be made, the people of Jakarta find a way to make it, no matter the place or time.

Not long after the amplified prayers from Jakarta's mosques have faded, the roar of traffic builds in intensity. The bus station at Blok M in the southern suburb of Kebayoran Baru becomes a confusion of people, buses, *mikrolets* and vans, all seemingly setting out at the same time in a mad yet congenial dash towards the city's core. The dash rapidly slows to an excruciating crawl, even on the eight lanes of Jalan Jenderal Sudirman, as it nears the jammed cloverleaf intersection with Jalan Gatot Subroto. Youngsters bravely wade into the traffic selling the latest issue of *Tempo*, a

**More than 90 per cent** *of the Indonesian people are Muslims. The national Istiqlal Mosque on Medan Merdeka* **(Freedom Field)** *is a major focus of Islamic worship in the country and amplified songs from its minaret call Jakarta's Muslims to prayer.*

*The leader responsible for the rapid economic growth of Jakarta and the rest of the Indonesian nation of some 13,677 islands is President Suharto. Schoolboys walk past a visage of the "Father of Development" that adorns one of the patriotic billboards put up around Medan Merdeka during the National Day festivities held throughout the island republic on August 17 each year.*

weekly newsmagazine, and hawking the morning newspapers to people of the nation.

The rivers of vehicles inch past small squares of *padi* cultivated right in the shadow of mighty glass and chrome skyscrapers: past brooding monuments and lush parks and grease-colored canals, through wide avenues shaded by arching tamarinds and fringed with gracious mansions, down narrow arteries hemmed with open drains and rows of humble,

ly as an oil spill, spreading across the coastal plains to the east and west, creeping up the slopes of the volcanic bulge of mountains to the south. Even in the seas to the north, the "Thousand Islands" have been enveloped as recreational suburbs of the city.

The populace of this shapeless metropolis averages 10,000 every square kilometer and 25,000 in the core of the city. The total population is conservatively estimated at

attached adobe dwellings draped with children, into the heart of Jakarta — Southeast Asia's largest, most populous city, capital of Indonesia, the world's fifth most populous nation, gateway to an archipelago of 13,677 islands of impenetrable jungles, ancient monuments, fuming volcanos and endless summers.

Jakarta is an amalgam of the moods and nuances of this vast archipelago. Surveyors put the size of the city at approximately 650 square kilometers, two-and-a-half times that of the whole of Singapore, the island nation to the northwest. It is an estimate, however, that was undoubtedly being exceeded even as it was made. Jakarta is expanding as fast and aimless-

*Jakarta's sidewalks, byways and streets are all part of a huge and sprawling urban bazaar of unusual goods and services. This particular wheel of commerce has arrived with cages full of curious* ayam, *or chickens, bound for city pots.*

seven million, representing most of the myriad of races, religions and cultures of the nation's islands. But every year thousands of newborns swell that figure, and newcomers from elsewhere in Java and the archipelago flock to the city as they would run to the warm embrace of their excited mother.

In fact, Indonesians call Jakarta their *Ibukota,* "Mother City." And it does exude a kind of maternal magnetism. Spread across a triangular alluvium, its rich red earth is improbably fertile. Orchids, jasmine, bougainvilleas, banyans and infinite varieties of vegetation thrive. The rapid encroachment of concrete is no deterrent. Construction workers returning to building projects that have lain fallow for a while have found veritable forests growing in the lobbies. Jakarta has also proven a fertile ground for ideas. It is a center of learning and art, entertainment and high society, as well as the nation's administrative nucleus.

It is to the heart of this hub that the tens of thousands flock every day. Jakarta's traffic, a certain sign of progress, snarls and slows early every morning (except Sunday when the jams shift to roads leading out of the city) and stays that way most of the day. An ubiquitous corps of parking attendants exacerbates the problem. At virtually every curbside carpark, these self-employed *parkirs* accept a handout of 100

endure, another of the facets that give Jakarta the atmosphere of a vast, unending bazaar. "*Tidak apa-apa*," the Indonesians say. "Never mind. There's no sense in worrying about it." The Indonesians' rational attitude to life is one that other countries would do well to emulate.

If there is a lull in the frenzy at all, it occurs at midday when the energy-sapping equatorial sun washes the color out of the urban landscape and many people withdraw for prayer,

rupiah for guiding motorists into a tight spot with shouts of "*terus, terus*" ("come on, come on"). Unfortunately, they don't always yell "*stop*" (which has the same meaning in Indonesian as it does in English) in time to prevent the driver from depositing his fender in the door of another parked vehicle.

Although they do not have *polisi* badges, some *parkirs* even halt oncoming traffic to wave cars in and out of parking spaces to earn their 100 rupiah, further ensnarling traffic and sometimes causing accidents. The chairman of Jakarta's parking authority has complained that *parkirs* have become a "social problem". But intensified efforts to control them by licensing official *parkirs* and arresting unlicensed ones have not succeeded in curtailing their activities. Like the *becak* pedicabs that officials have been trying to banish from the city for years, *parkirs* appear destined to

lunch or a catnap. Yet when the late afternoon shadows grow and cover the city in darkness and the last of the day's prayer calls echo and fade away, the people of Jakarta get their second wind. They socialize or shop at the night markets that spring up everywhere. The sidewalks along main thoroughfares glow with dozens of kerosene lamps that illuminate blankets and knee-high tables where *kakilima* (literally, five-footers), display a mind-boggling array of merchandise within just about that miniscule amount of space.

The well-to-do head for the Hilton to disco or to Chinese nightclubs and dance halls along Jalan Hayam Wuruk, or at the Taman Impian

*When boys grow up, many still enjoy working on the street corners — as traffic policemen. Like most rapidly growing cities, Jakarta has its share of modern urban ills, including smog, overpopulation and massive rush hour traffic jams.*

Ancol amusement complex (appropriately, it means "Dreamland"), where they cha cha, foxtrot and gyrate to the local dance craze, the *joget*. Of course, there is always the time and the wherewithal to cap the night off with a bowl of *bubur ayam*, spicy chicken porridge, at the Hotel Indonesia coffee shop.

One journalist, writing in *Berita Buana*, called Jakarta a "restless city that stays awake 24 hours". He continued: "To sleep soundly here is somewhat unlikely since from daybreak to dusk till day again, people can hardly stay home ... its residents roam about the city the whole day and night. Streets, alleys, parks and public places are all occupied and heavily congested nearly all the time. And there is always noise, which is a nuisance to those who want to take a nap or sleep."

**M**ost of life's mundane activities for most of the people of Jakarta occur in the

*kampung*, the virtually self-contained little villages within the city, isolated from the main streets and from each other by solid walls of miniature residences, one cemented up against the next. The only thoroughfares in most *kampungs* are concrete or earthen footpaths, just wide enough to accommodate motorbikes and *becaks*. They are bordered on either side by drains, sometimes used as lavatories by the crowds of children whose ubiquity (40 per cent of the population of Indonesia was under the age of 15 in 1985) is rivaled only by that of squawking chickens (the so-called *ayam kampung* — chicken — is scrawny and tough but far more tasty than the protein-fattened chick-

*Socializing is one of the most popular pastimes of Jakarta's gregarious people. Women, clad in the traditional* sarong kebaya, *swap gossip while picnicking under a palm (**left**) and students chat on the portico of the Fine Arts Museum.*

en of the West). From the air, Jakarta's acres of *kampungs* look like a giant maze (the kind you roll a marble around while trying to keep it from disappearing down a hole) with the paths delineated by the tiles on the red slate rooftops — and no readily apparent outlet.

Jakarta would not be Jakarta without its *kampungs*. A colorful patchwork of hundreds of them, all shapes and sizes, gives the city a distinctive atmosphere that exists nowhere else in the world. *Kampungs* are often erroneously believed by many newcomers to be squatter slums of makeshift hovels nailed together from scraps of plywood and corrugated iron. Some are. The great majority are not. Most *kampungs* are simply congregations of the modest homes, shops, mosques, churches, schools and medical clinics of the average Jakartan and are surprisingly neat and tidy, considering the overwhelming numbers

of people packed into them.

Masses of people from rural Java and other islands began streaming into the *kampungs*, after independence from the Dutch in 1945. At that time, Batavia, the comparatively serene home of only about 200,000, became Jakarta, capital of the new Republic of Indonesia. By 1950, it grew to a million. People from the same islands or villages would often congregate in a single *kampung* where they could live with others of the same culture in the way to which they had been accustomed.

Over the years, the cultural distinctions between these cities-within-the-city have become blurred. Ardent Christians from Ambon

*A man who makes his living from the seat of his bicycle takes a breather from the midday heat (above) while a woman, protected from the intense equatorial sun by a hat, cools off her merchandise at Pasar Ikan, the Fish Market (right).*

**Indonesia's traditional herbal remedies,** collectively called *jamu*, are stacked on the shelves of stores and street vendors. They come in a wide variety of brands that claim to provide relief for virtually every affliction known to man.

# The Joys of Jamu

Centuries ago, Javanese women who lived behind the intrigue-laden walls of Central Java's royal courts developed a natural method for maintaining their beauty, vigor and vitality. They blended delicately balanced herbs and spices in special formulas that they called jamu.

Today, a bewildering variety of jamu sold under an equally bewildering variety of brand names are used by Indonesians in all walks of life, from housewives to laborers. In fact, the Indonesian Ministry of Health estimates that 80 per cent of the nation's 160 million people have snipped open a colorful packet of medicinal herbs and downed the national health drink — strong, bitter concoctions — quickly, at least once in their lives. Many endure the ritual every day.

Familiar names like Air Mancur, Nyona Meneer and Jamu Jago and equally familiar trademarks like a crowing cock, waterfalls and the portrait of a long-haired woman with a silky complexion, cover advertising billboards on buses and roadsides all over Jakarta. Although many of these major names in the production of jamu have their headquarters in Central Java, where the traditions and origins of jamu are firmly rooted, the capital city also has its share of small-scale factories.

One of them is Jamu Darmi, operated by Ibu (Mrs.) Suparto. "Our forefathers were not stupid," she says. "They knew that what was needed to preserve good health and keep in condition was easily acquired from the nature that surrounds us."

Ibu Suparto is living proof of her product's amazing properties. Although she is approaching her seventies, she has the soft skin of a young lady, a result she says of years of using her special jamu preparations. Some are applied externally, others swallowed. The family recipes have been passed down to her through many generations. And even while she is speaking, she casually rubs her face with a few leaves freshly-picked from a garden she calls her "living drugstore".

"These leaves help prevent wrinkling and are a lot cheaper than all those fancy new creams made by the big synthetic cosmetic companies," she says, revealing another reason for the popularity of jamu among the Indonesian masses. The vast majority of the population cannot afford to buy imported cosmetics, vitamins and health preparations.

Ibu Suparto's small cottage industry in suburban Jakarta brings in 60 kinds of roots, flowers, bark, nuts and herbs from fields in East Java and other Indonesian islands. She also has her own garden of special ingredients. Plants are immediately dried in the sun or ovens to keep them from becoming moldy, then pulverized and blended into the various "secret" formulas of her ancestors and, just as importantly,

those she has developed herself.

"Besides being a substitute for aspirin, vitamin pills and cold tablets, this totally natural herbal medicine tackles such complaints as asthma, acne, baldness, diarrhoea, leprosy, malaria, venereal disease, piles and high blood pressure," Ibu Suparto says — with an air of nonchalance.

Some forms of jamu are marketed as aphrodisiacs, not always tastefully, while others reputedly have the ability to ease the strain on those who enjoy an active sex life. The industry has grown into an economic powerhouse over the past few decades and jamu is now available in powders, capsules, pills, liquids, pastes and creams. The common denominator is that all the diverse brands are guaranteed to contain 100 per cent natural ingredients.

Mass-marketed by companies like Jamu Darmi, jamu has become a multi-million dollar industry. But there is also a thriving trade in herbal potions right at the street level. Jamu ladies, formally dressed in traditional kain blouse and sarong kebaya, ply Jakarta's streets, in exclusive residential districts and the kampungs, with home-brewed remedies stored in an array of Johnny Walker bottles which they carry slung over their shoulders.

While the trade in jamu for males has burgeoned, Indonesian women are still the main consumers. Most remember their mothers forcing them to swallow unpalatable liquid jamu as an all-purpose tonic, just as Western children decades ago cringed as they swallowed doses of castor oil.

When a women matures, jamu is there to insure that she will be radiant, beautiful and irresistible to her husband on her wedding day. Weeks in advance of the big event, her body is anointed with the popular, sweet-smelling lulur paste. Made from rice powder, it is applied with coconut milk (for dry skin), water and jasmine or rose petals (for normal skin) and aged tamarind (for oily skin). Brides say the treatment makes the skin fragrant and irresistibly cool to the touch.

Visitors wishing to sample the joys that jamu may bring will find many salons in Jakarta offering "full-service" beauty treatments. Mustika Ratu, Jalan K.H. Wahid Hasyim 133 (Tel. 343–585) is one of the most popular and offers an up-market line of cosmetics manufactured from natural products.

Ibu Moorjati Soedibjo, the radiantly attractive owner of Mustika Ratu, says the salon offers special treatments like wraps with special flowers to firm the skin, herbal powders to flatten the stomach, saunas with the vapor of fragrant sirih leaves and herbal cream baths that strengthen the hair.

And for those wishing to smooth wrinkled skin, and who can stand the thought of it, the salon offers a unique form of facial — with seaweed.

27

live peaceably in the same lane where strict Muslims from Aceh walk to the mosque. But many of the subdivisions are still referred to by names that reveal the heritage of their first settlers: Kampung Arab, Kampung Aceh, Kampung Bali and Kampung Makassar, to name just a few examples.

Although more and more office towers and a few tall condominiums are rising above the *kampungs*, the people of Jakarta seem to prefer living in dense concentrations on the ground, to the prospect of life in the kind of highrises that have been built to house those with modest incomes in other developing countries. The director of the city's Kampung Improvement Program, Darrundono, once explained to a regional news magazine that "in Java people have always lived on the ground; it's important to them". Even in increasingly urban Jakarta, people still prefer to feel their roots firmly embedded in the nourishing earth.

No visit to Jakarta is complete without at least a stroll through one of its bustling *kampungs*. The best way to visit for the uninitiated who do not speak Indonesian, is by nurturing friendships — with hotel or restaurant staff, business associates, even taxi drivers. It often proves only a matter of a brief meeting or two before they extend a sincere invitation to their home, particularly during the weeks following the *Lebaran* holiday that marks the end of the Islamic fasting season, *Idul Fitri*. (At that time, even President Suharto throws opens his doors to all and anyone willing to wait in the long lines can exchange greetings with him and his wife, Madame Tien, at their residential compound on Jalan Cendana in the Menteng district).

Otherwise, simply ask an Indonesian friend or associate to take you through a *kampung*. More often than not they will take you to their own and it will culminate in a visit to their home where you will be treated to peanuts, crispy *krupuk* wafers made from prawns or crabs or colorful snacks like *kueh getuk* and *kueh dodol* which are made from eggs, rice flour, tapioca and sugar, and are gooey but pleasant tasting. For drinks there will probably be *teh botel*, a popular bottled tea, or *air jeruk*, concentrated fruit juice mixed with water that is usually so sweet it will make your teeth tingle and your eyes water.

---

*Crowded, tightly-packed clusters of simple dwellings are the patchwork neighborhoods that comprise Jakarta. Canals built by Dutch colonials homesick for Amsterdam still provide transpor-tation networks in some kampungs.*

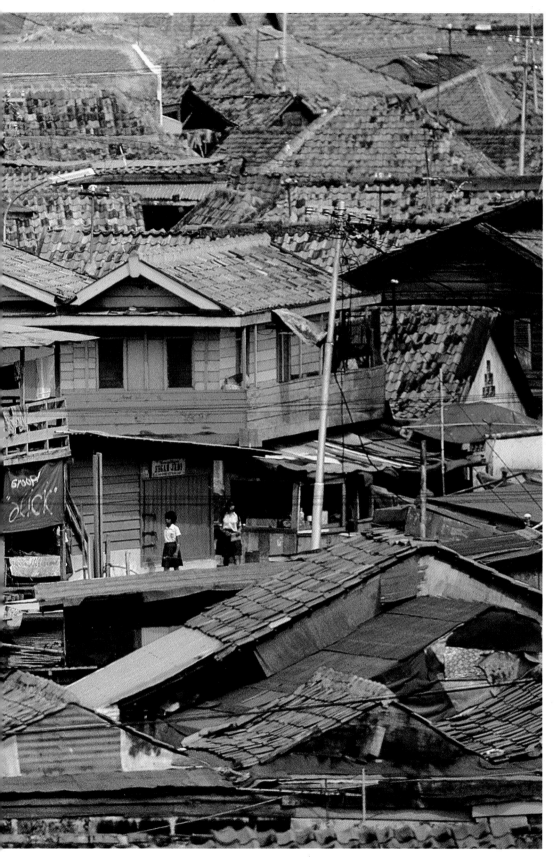

***An alternative to getting around*** the city by bus or taxi is the squat, three-wheeled motorized vehicle known as the bajaj. Caravans of bajaj (the people of Jakarta call them "bajai") ply the side streets of the capital but are barred from Jakarta's many major roads.

**Life as a becak driver** is increasingly difficult in Jakarta as the hand-scrawled words on the front of this driver's pedicab poignantly reveals. The sign reads: "This is the hardship I endure."

# The Incredible Vanishing Becak

The becak *has been one of the quintessential elements of Jakarta's incongruous urban landscape for decades. Legions of these three-wheeled pedicabs ply the side streets and back alleys of the city, piloted from behind the passenger seat by wiry men hunched in a jockey's crouch. Splashed with bright painted patterns, they provide a colorful, inexpensive means of getting around.*

*In outlying cities of Java, especially Yogyakarta, the thousands of* becaks *that race past stalled automobiles and thread their way through traffic jams are indispensable facts of life. In modern, progressive Jakarta, however, the* becak *is an anomaly, a remnant of times when the number of buses and taxis were few and the economy was in a shambles and an unpleasant reminder of even earlier colonial times when the Dutch men and women passengers were elephantine (by Indonesian standards). Explains the present day vice governor of Jakarta. "We must rid our city of the* becak *because it is the last example of man exploiting man."*

Becaks *are also considered a hazard to motor vehicles and an impediment to smooth traffic flow that could hamper the city's development. So a campaign to systematically rid Jakarta of* becaks *began in 1972 when they were banned from the main thoroughfares. Most drivers simply began using side streets, confining their routes to limited areas that did not traverse the prohibited streets, or operated clandestinely under the cover of night.*

*As Jakarta's population continued to swell with unskilled people from rural areas, so did the number of* becak *drivers and potential passengers, regardless of the official ban. So city officials tried tougher measures. They required all drivers, known as* tukang becak *or "one skilled in the art of* becak *driving," to obtain operators' permits. But that did not faze the drivers either. In early 1986, city officials reported that only 7,800 of an estimated 80,000* becak *drivers operating in the city had valid licenses.*

*Throwing up their hands, city officials finally implemented a total ban on Jakarta's pedicabs that same year. They followed up that move with action, staging several sweeps in which thousands of pedicabs were confiscated and dumped in Jakarta Bay to serve as artificial reefs. Still the sunken* becak *reappeared on the streets, waterlogged and rusty but in working order. They had been located, then hooked and reeled in by enterprising fishermen who resold them to their original owners.*

*One Indonesian journalist, writing in the* Jakarta Post, *attributes the resilience of the* becak *to the simple fact that "it still fills a need for transportation of the common man". Not only is it the only vehicle small enough to thread its way through the narrow lanes of many of the city's densely-populated quar-*

*ters, but it is the only means of travel for the many Jakartans who cannot afford cab fares.*

*Those facts do not appear to be readily apparent to some of the* becak's *foes in the city administration. Asked how low-income housewives returning from a shopping trip are supposed to get their heavy bundles from the bus stop to their homes deep in the kampung, one municipal government official replied truculently, "Let them take taxis."*

*As in most of the free world, the automobile has become the preferred means of transportation in Jakarta for those who can afford it. In actuality, it is the motor vehicle — not the* becak *— that is the true nemesis of Jakarta's highways. According to police Colonel Sentot Roemekso, head of the police department's directorate of traffic control, there are more than 1.2 million cars, trucks, vans, buses and taxis using the capital's 4,500 kilometers of roads; lined up end-to-end with only 10 centimeters between each bumper, the number of vehicles in Jakarta would stretch from Jakarta to East Timor.*

*Another consideration in the* becak *dilemma is Jakarta's unemployment problem. Most drivers are unskilled immigrants who hail from other parts of Indonesia. They earn only about Rp4,000 a day pedaling passengers around, about half of which goes to lease the* becak *from its owner. But that is still more than they would make back in their villages.*

*Since overheads are low — they sleep in their* becaks *or in the owners' dormitories and eat at food stalls — drivers save enough money to send home to their families for education and other needs. Says one 35-year-old* tukang becak *named Darso, "My children are in school, so when they grow up my sons won't have to work as* becak *drivers."*

*Another enterprising driver named Sarjono made the jump from driving* becaks *to driving hire cars. He's putting his sons through high school.*

*Some officials fear that putting the* becak *out of business is tantamount to putting tens of thousands of their countrymen out of work. While their children may grow up educated and able to find better jobs in skilled fields and professions, few* becak *drivers themselves are likely to make a successful transition to another kind of employment.*

*Such considerations have undoubtedly been reflected in City Hall's reluctance to enforce its anti-becak laws more rigidly. Whether the durable* becak *and its drivers continue to endure efforts to banish them from every corner of Jakarta remains to be seen. In the meantime, the adventurous visitor will discover that a swift cool ride aboard a* becak *through the silent streets of the city after midnight, past the night people, under arching tamarinds, mellowed by the tropical moon, remains one of Jakarta's many delights.*

Failing all that, simply ask a taxi driver to drop you at the beginning of one of the many paths in Jakarta that seem to lead nowhere — and walk down it. The immense *kampung* near the Pasar Baru shopping district is particularly large and fascinating. Once inside, you will be overwhelmed by the warmth and hospitality of the Indonesians. You will emerge with a new outlook on life and the concepts of neighborliness and goodwill.

The *lurah*, or *kampung* headman, routinely assembles neighborhood teams to clean up in the aftermath of a storm or flood and even to lend a hand in improvement programs. People receive no hard cash for their hard work, but are content that they have contributed to the betterment of their community.

The *kampungs*, like all units and levels of Indonesian society, also employ a principle called *musjawarah* that comes into play in the

Indonesians are unusually gregarious, a trait that undoubtedly helps them live together in relative harmony in the densely-crowded *kampungs* despite the constant heat, noise and clutter. Certainly poverty and crime exist as they do in all big cities. But an old philosophy called *gotong royong* that has guided the people in many Indonesian islands still appears to work in the *kampungs* of Jakarta.

*Gotong royong* is simply an institutionalized mutual cooperation policy. People in the *kampungs* of Jakarta, like those in rural villages of Java, feel personally responsible for each other and for each other's families. In a personal crisis, like a death in the *kampung*, neighbors are there to console grieving relatives and even assist with funeral arrangements. On happy occasions, like weddings, they pitch in and lend a hand to help prepare meals and welcome guests from elsewhere.

event that a dispute does arise. It calls for the problem to be resolved through mutual discussion and conferences that are presided over by a mediator. *Musjawarah* leads to a consensus or mutual agreement, *mufakat*, that permits peaceful settlement of the dispute. On a higher plane, Indonesia's system of government operates on the democratic principles of *musjawarah* and *mufakat*.

Of course, the pressures of contemporary life, with its emphasis on "getting ahead" and "keeping up with the Achmads", have been whittling away traditional influences including *gotong royong* and *musjawarah* and *mufakat*. But it is a tribute to the moral fiber of the

*One of the exciting facets of the city is its vibrant street life, from self-styled chefs who dish up Indonesian specialities from pushcarts (left) to the legions of becak drivers (above) who still pedal their painted vehicles in some parts of town.*

average Indonesian that such time-honored concepts are still important. For they make life more pleasant for all in even the poorest parts of Jakarta and have engendered a spirit of hospitality that is becoming legendary. It is a spirit that is not lost on Western visitors and expatriates who live and work in the city.

"People are friendly and that makes all the difference," says Michael Scheutzendorf, a German who has worked with hundreds of

been in its modern history.

Most significant has been a concerted effort by the New Order administration of President Suharto to improve the quality of life for the millions who live in Jakarta's urban villages. By the middle of the 1980s, the city had spent 107 billion rupiah, roughly the equivalent of U.S.$100 million, improving 537 new and 82 rehabilitated *kampungs* that are home to nearly five million people. The government

Jakartans as general manager of the Jakarta Hilton. "Whenever I'm in Germany I perform an exercise in futility. I start counting the number of people I see or meet that are smiling or laughing. I can count them on the fingers of one hand. When I do it here, I run out of hands and fingers."

What the city of Jakarta lacks in physical comfort and beauty is more than compensated for by the warmth and beauty of its people.

While the physical appearance of Jakarta has rarely been one of its attractions, the city has taken on a more pleasing countenance in recent years. In fact, the Indonesian capital is probably cleaner and greener than it has ever

*Foreign visitors need not understand the Indonesian language as Jakarta's people often communicate more with a facial expression than a linguist can with words — as do the bemused lady (above) and the congenial hotel doorman (right).*

constructed roads, bridges, drains and other water channels, built and outfitted first aid clinics, community health centers and schools and has trained paramedics.

The addition of more communal bathing and washing facilities, purification of water through deep-well pumps, construction of more water hydrants and restoration and extension of water pipe networks has helped improve sanitation. More than 130 kilometers of spanking new arterial roads and 525 kilometers of local roads were constructed, the output of potable water was increased to reach more than half of the city's residents and more than 300,000 government-subsidized, low cost homes were built.

To its credit, the government has attempted to preserve existing structures of historical importance wherever possible (rather than bulldozing everything and rebuilding), to

maintain the city's integrity and character. Some structures date back well into the Dutch colonial era. In some cases, contemporary architects have also incorporated local influences in their building designs.

For example, the terminal buildings of the airy Soekarno-Hatta International Airport, which opened on the city's outskirts in 1985, are topped with traditional sloping roofs of terracotta tiles. The interiors are finished with dark wood ceilings and halls that showcase Indonesian arts and crafts. Connecting corridors that are open to the sultry tropical breezes look out on landscaped green corridors and, beyond that, to even greener *sawah*, the rice fields that carpet much of Java.

Incredibly, the beautification of Jakarta has been accomplished in less than two decades. For all his charisma and success in uniting the Indonesian people under one flag and instilling in them a sense of identity, the Republic's first President, Sukarno, left behind serious economic problems when he lost control of the country's destiny in 1965. Nowhere was the evidence of economic chaos greater than in Jakarta where public funds were squandered on monuments and other frills while the city's infrastructure deteriorated.

Despite the most obvious examples of progress — the sweeping, clean highways, office towers and landscaped parks — much of the city still appears to have been pasted together haphazardly in a curious collage that could be described — kindly — as abstract. That is because it was. The pace of planning has not kept up with the pace of the city's expansion. New *kampungs* still take root in the fertile red Javanese soil. They grow rapidly, dropping roots from ever-expanding branches much like the mighty, sprawling banyan trees that are so much a part of the city's tropical jungle trimmings.

Even on a major street in one of the city's wealthy enclaves, the unbridled growth has made it frustrating to locate an address. A single avenue may have several bungalows with the same house number while there appears to be no logic or sequence to the numbers on other gates. Number 34 may come between 62 and 180; number 89b between 46b and 3. "People like to choose their own house numbers. What can we do?" explained one

*The distinctive culture of Jakarta is called Betawi, an Indonesianized pronunciation of the old Dutch name for the city. Giant ondel-ondel figures, a delightful part of Betawi tradition, delight youngsters at Taman Impian Ancol.*

# A Puppet for All Seasons

**P**uppetry has always been a popular form of entertainment in Indonesia, as well as an integral part of its culture. Wayang kulit, *shadow puppets intricately hand-tooled in leather, are the most common form. Highly-trained puppet masters, cal-*led dalangs, *skilfully put* wayang kulit *through their paces behind screens lit with kerosene lanterns in Jakarta's* kampungs *and in villages throughout Java. Large audiences, alternately watching and dozing, attend the performances that often continue until dawn's light consumes the shadowy figures.*

Wayang golek *are beautifully-carved and painted wooden puppets that click and clack their way through tales from the Ramayana, Mahabarata and other Hindu epics. Human dancers and actors often look like puppets themselves when they don masks, called* wayang topeng, *with the faces of beautiful princesses and handsome princes or grotesque mons-ters and deformed people.*

*Jakarta's Betawi culture has its* ondel-ondel, *towering dolls made from wood and paper that lead wedding processions, emcee at the city's birthday parades each June 22, add to the festive atmosphere at Jakarta's Disneyland, Dunia Fantasie, and turn up, ostensibly, at other events in the city.*

*Jakarta, the center of Indonesia's entertainment* industry, produces hundreds of movies, music cas-settes, and other modern diversions, annually. Yet even here, puppetry still plays a major role in society, though with a decidedly contemporary look, in the form of the popular character Si Unyil.

*Si Unyil is a puppet that embodies Indonesian youth in the shape of an eight-year-old primary schoolboy. Although he is not even human, Si Unyil is the star of an Indonesian television series of the same name that has become one of the nation's highest-rated programs since its introduction in 1979.*

*As the son of a farmer living in a fictional village called Sukamaju, which translates as "on the way to progress", Si Unyil serves as a role model, in much the same way the* wayang *puppet has throughout Indonesian history. The big difference is that through the medium of television, his message reaches an incredibly vast audience. Granted, performances of traditional* wayang kulit *and* wayang golek *are occasionally shown on television. But Si Unyil has his own weekly 20-minute series.*

*Even villagers in such remote islands as Banda Neira, in the southern Moluccas, and in remote jungles in Irian Jaya and Kalimantan can be found crowding around the neighborhood television set in a market or the village headman's home, eyes glued to*

BAZAAR SENI RUPA
KOPERASI
SENIMAN INDONESIA

**Wayang Golek,** the art of bringing traditional wooden puppets to life, is still a popular form of entertainment in Indonesia (**left**). However, a contemporary puppet named Si Unyil and his friends and family (**below**), developed by the country's Jakarta-based national television network, reach a massive audience every week.

the adventures of Si Unyil. The shows are so popular that the streets of many cities and villages are often deserted during Sunday morning broadcasts.

The character was developed in 1979 by Kurnain Suhardiman and Suyadi. Around their ideal Indonesian boy they created a cast of complementary characters who help in conveying the show's moral messages. Unyil's dad is forever instructing children to be responsible citizens while his friend, Pak Raden, represents traditional Javanese thinking. Si Unyil's band of playmates includes Melani, a girl of Chinese descent, who encourages assimilation and acceptance of Indonesia's Chinese minority. Pak Lurah, the respected village headman, urges Si Unyil and other youngsters to make positive contributions to the development of their community. Rounding out the cast are the penjahat, criminal characters who provide dramatic tension but in the happy ending, of course, always get caught and punished.

Each episode of Si Unyil focuses on a national problem or issue and provides a practical lesson for the young — and old — audiences. For example, one episode, entitled Guests from Abroad, provided practical advice on how to be hospitable to foreign travelers. An important lesson in light of Indonesia's burgeoning tourist industry in which adventurous visitors often stray into communities that may have had limited contact with foreign people and customs.

Another Si Unyil episode, The Total Sun Eclipses, dispelled lingering fears among some Indonesians that the sun would be swallowed by a malevolent giant during a total solar eclipse in June, 1983. Even more obvious were the messages of shows called Shamed Because of Lying, The Wisdom of Saving, and Clean is Healthy.

To the casual observer, even those who do not understand Indonesian, the Si Unyil show might appear to be a simple undertaking. But, like the wayang kulit performances from which it is derived the production is a complex undertaking. About 30 writers, artists and assistants are involved in producing each episode for the state-owned Pusat Produksi Film Negara, an arm of the Ministry of Information. Information Minister Harmoko has attributed the popularity of Si Unyil to the fact that his actions are "strictly rooted in our national values and identity."

Like most modern media stars, Si Unyil's fame has grown far beyond that of his weekly program. Puppeteers now take the television characters on the road, playing "live" show. Si Unyil has even been in demand by Kodak, Unilever and Peter's Ice Cream, for their advertising campaigns.

frustrated city official who looked perplexed.

Streets often change name as they run on their meandering course through the city. Jalan Iman Bonjol, for instance, suddenly turns into Jalan Diponegoro after rounding a bend. Jalan M.H. Thamrin even more suddenly becomes Jalan Jenderal Sudirman after passing under the pedestrian bridge in front of Hotel Kartika Plaza.

Indeed, it may come as a surprise to most newcomers to Jakarta that there is any systematic structure whatsoever underlying the apparent confusion of the capital. In fact, administratively, the city is divided into 30 districts, *kecematan*, and 236 subdistricts called *keluruhan*. Furthermore, each of the *keluruhan* are composed of ward organizations called *rukun tetangga*, or simply "R.T.'s".

According to Soedarmadji Damais, one of the members of the City Hall team who has

played a major role in restoration projects, the R.T.'s are one of the positive legacies of the occupation by Japan's 16th Army during World War II. When they marched into the city, the Japanese brought along their *tonari gumi*, self-governing districts to bring order to the disorganized sprawl. "Our present R.T.'s evolved from the *tonari gumi*," says Adji.

Jakarta's immensity alone makes it daunting. To put its growth and present character into perspective, it must be approached systematically. The best way to do that is to examine the city chronologically from its earliest beginnings to the development of its contemporary suburbs.

*Jakarta's importance as a port began centuries ago in Sunda Kelapa. Today, it's still a meeting place for dockworkers (left), crew (above) and the handbuilt sailing schooners of the archipelago's seafaring Bugis ethnic group (following pages)*

HET STADHUYS

BATAVIA.

**The city hall built by the Dutch** in 1710 has been restored by the metropolitan government along with other buildings in the Old Batavia district. Today the building, looking much as it did in this early ink engraving, houses the Jakarta Historical Museum. The Dutch building is a popular national landmark.

# Historical Chronology

**Hindu Period (to 1527)**

**5th Century** — To commemorate the digging of a canal, King Purnawarman erects a memorial stone where the northeast Jakarta enclave of Tugu now stands, evidence that then, as today, the area was prone to flooding. Purnawarman's Hindu kingdom, Taruma, indicates that organized settlements had existed in the vicinity for quite some time, an observation reinforced by the notes of the 5th century Chinese world traveler, Fa Hsien.

**1512** — The first Europeans, Portuguese merchants, sail into the port of Sunda Kelapa, northwest of Tugu, already a busy entrepôt of the syncretic Hindu-Buddhist kingdom of Sunda.

**1522** — The Portuguese sign a treaty of friendship with Sunda. The treaty permits them to erect a godown and fort in the harbor at Sunda Kelapa, downriver from Pajajaran, the seat of the Sundanese Kingdom. Pajajaran's political authorities believe the alliance with Portugal will help fortify their position against the growing might of neighboring Muslim sultanates. To honor the occasion, a large stone or *padrao*, now in the National Museum, is erected on the coast.

**Jayakarta Period (1527–1619)**

**1527** — The Portuguese fail to muster the expected military support and Sunda Kelapa is mowed down by the invading forces of the Central Javanese Kingdom of Demak and its Muslim leader Fatahillah, also known as Falatehan. Prince Fatahillah establishes Jayakarta (meaning "Glorious Victory") on the ashes of Sunda Kelapa on June 22. The world's maps call the city Jacatra.

**1596** — The first Dutch expedition, led by Admiral Cornelis de Houtman, visits the ports at Banten and Jayakarta in search of a hub from which the merchants can fortify their increasingly lucrative trade with the Moluccas, the "Spice Islands", in the eastern part of the archipelago.

**1598–99** — A second Dutch expedition ships cargos of pepper, mace and nutmeg to Holland via Jayakarta and Banten. The cargos earn these early adventurers a 400 per cent profit.

**1610** — Encouraged by increasing trade, the Dutch obtain permission to build a godown in the Chinese section of town on the east shore of the Ciliwung River, not far from the waterfront. The small commercial operation later evolves into the Nassau and Mauritius warehouses.

**1618** — The Dutch break the rules of their tenancy agreement with the Prince of Jayakarta by transforming the Nassau and Mauritius godowns into a well-fortified, solid stone fort that becomes known as Kasteel Jacatra. Meanwhile, the rival British increase their presence in the port with the support of the nervous prince — but to the annoyance of the Dutch merchants and navy.

*Old Dutch warships stand guard in the harbor of Batavia, the flourishing capital of the Dutch East Indies, in a 17th century engraving (left). The Dutch colonists imported Chinese coolies like the one in this 18th century painting (below) to do menial work.*

## The Colonial Period (1619–1945)

**1619** — Governor-General Jan Pieterszoon Coen of the United Dutch East India Company, the VOC, invades Jayakarta, levels it, makes it company property, then rebuilds it along the lines of the low-lying towns of the Netherlands complete with canals and walls. The Kasteel is further strengthened and renamed Batavia in honor of his country's area of Germanic ancestors.

Batavia eventually comes into common usage as the name of the entire settlement. The bastions of the fort are named after gemstones, a nomenclature responsible for Batavia's 17th century reputation as the "City of Jewels" and "Pearl of the Orient". Coen uses the city as the base of operations for driving the British and other European competitors from the archipelago. As the headquarters for the VOC's trading empire, Coen makes Batavia one of the most powerful cities of the colonial era.

**1620** — A hastily-built City Hall is erected 500 meters inland from the kasteel of Batavia.

**1628–29** — Sultan Agung of the Central Java kingdom of Mataram sends 80,000 men against Batavia in two separate, unsuccessful assaults. According to an old account, a Dutch garrison fought off one attack by dumping the contents of freshly-utilized latrine buckets on the heads of their enemies. Although victorious, the Dutch further strengthened the walls around the city to discourage future attacks. On the night of September 21, 1629, Coen dies at the age of 42, an apparent victim of cholera, one of the deadly diseases fostered by Dutch neglect of Batavia's worsening sanitary conditions. He was buried in Batavia, but the site of his grave has been lost to the ravages of time and memory. Appropriately, it is rumored to be under the foundations of a warehouse.

**1632** — An urban administration is institutionalized by the appointment of a council of aldermen. A new and more permanent City Hall is built.

**1648** — Phoa Bigam, an enterprising Chinese sea captain, digs a canal from the old walled city, *Oud Batavia*, to what today is Jalan Veteran to facilitate commercial transport of raw materials from the hinterlands to the harbor. The canal, later called the Molenvliet, spurs the growth of the *Nieuw Batavia* beyond the walls in an area called Weltevreden located to the city's south.

**1650** — Other industrious Chinese residents, who account for 30 per cent of the city's population, build fortunes in agriculture, commerce, shipping, banking, construction and other fields and become increasingly influential. They build Buddhist temples, called *klenteng*, in the vicinity of modern Glodok and Ancol around which a thriving Chinatown takes shape. Dutch residents of Batavia engage in ostentatious displays of their wealth by building estates and parading through the streets in silk, linen, gold, silver and diamonds.

**1652** — The *Westzijdsche Pakhuizan*, a row of warehouses, is constructed on the west bank of the Ciliwung River near the harbor. The buildings are filled to overflowing with pepper, tea, coffee and cotton. Today, they house the Museum Bahari.

**1683** — Old Sultan Abulfatah Agung of Banten incites an ill-fated insurrection against Batavia. The Dutch feed 5,000 of the survivors of the Banten War to the crocodiles in the river. As a consequence, Batavia gains total control of West Java.

**1700** — Batavia, population about 50,000, is not only in control of most of Java but many of modern Indonesia's outer islands as well. The city reaches the peak of its prestige and power and becomes known as the "Queen of the East". Textiles and pepper from Sumatra begin to exceed the economic importance of spices from the Moluccas.

**1710** — A third City Hall is completed after three years of construction and inaugurated on January 23 by Governor-General Abraham von Riebeeck. It becomes the adminstrative heart of the VOC, which is beginning to feel the economic strains of managing its far-flung island empire. Today, the sturdy building houses the Jakarta City Museum.

**1722** — Pieter Eberveld, a wealthy Eurasian resident of Batavia, is accused of conspiring with a cult leader, Raden Kartadria, to incite the Javanese to kill all Dutch inhabitants of Batavia on New Year's Day in order to install himself as Tuan Goesti, the "Big Lord" of Batavia. Despite serious doubts about the authenticity of the accusation, Eberveld, Kartadria and their followers are found guilty and crucified, flayed, dismembered, and quartered during their gruesome executions outside the castle walls. A recent monument marking the sordid affair on Jalan Pangeran Jayakarta, not far from the old Portuguese Church, later replaced another erected at the time. No longer a pleasant and queenly place, Batavia earns the title *Graf der Hollanders,* "the sepulcher of the Dutch".

**1730** — Urban ills engulf Batavia: floods, squalid housing, poor sanitation give rise to outbreaks of disease that claim the lives of thousands of Dutch and local residents alike. "It is impossible to visit this city and not to be astonished at the pains that have been taken to unite in one spot all possible causes of disease," one visiting British bureaucrat would later write. The decay of the inner city accelerates the exodus to the expanding suburbs.

**1733** — Landowner Julius Vinck opens two huge markets — Pasar Senen (the Monday Market) and Pasar Tanah Abang (Red-Clay Market). He connects them with roads that were the first east-west thoroughfares in the city and that later became Jalan Kebon Sirih and Jalan Prapatan.

**1740** — Concerned about the growing influence, affluence and size of Batavia's Chinese population, and suspicious that some were involved in the alleged Eberveld plot, the Dutch administration begins deporting large numbers of Chinese immigrants, precipitating a violent backlash. Fearing Chinese inside the city would join in attacks on Dutch citizens that had occurred in the environs, Governor-General Adriaan Valckenier imposes a curfew on Chinatown and sends soldiers into the quarter in search of weapons. On October 9, shots are fired igniting a massacre. By some accounts, 10,000 Chinese men, women, children, even hospital patients are slaughtered. Fire rages through Chinatown for days destroying 700 homes. Some Dutch residents are so appalled, the Governor-General later resigns, is arrested and jailed for instigating the bloodshed. The massacre touches off nearly two decades of insurrection from the Chinese and Javanese throughout the island, adding to the problems of the floundering VOC.

**1751** — Valckenier dies in prison. A religious leader named Kyai Tapa leads a rebellion against Batavia from Banten and later terrorizes Europeans on the outskirts of the city. The population of Batavia by now exceeds 100,000.

**1753** — The VOC seizes control of Banten, snuffing

out further trouble from its Javanese leaders.

**1760** — As fears of wild animals and attacks from Bantam dissipate, wealthy Dutch traders build country estates outside the city walls and south Batavia begins to take shape.

**1762** — Bounty hunters kill 27 tigers and panthers around Batavia in return for booty.

**1775** — Protestant Minister Johannes Hooyman builds Pondok Gede estate, well south of Batavia on the road to Buitenzorg (modern Bogor). Coffee and tea grown in the Prianger region south of Batavia become increasingly important in trade.

**1778** — The exclusive Batavia Society of Arts and Sciences is founded by J.C. M. Radermacher. The Society's first collection consists of plants, animals, and so-called "freaks of nature " that were a phenomenon popular at the time.

**1795** — The Netherlands falls to Napoleon and a French protectorate is established. Prince William V flees to England, setting the stage for later changes in the government in Batavia.

**1797** — J.A. van Braam builds a grand country house on his Weltevreden estate. It later becomes the State Palace. The administrative and military center begins shifting from unhealthy Old Batavia to the New Batavia area of Weltevreden.

**1799** — With its debts totaling nearly 90 million guilders, and torn by high-level corruption, mismanagement and brutal policies toward native populations, the government of the French-occupied Netherlands dissolves the VOC by allowing its charter to expire. A colonial administration of the Netherlands East Indies is established in Batavia to replace the multinational's rule.

**1808** — Napoleon appoints a Dutchman with French connections and sympathies, Marshal Herman Willem Daendels, as Governor-General of the Netherlands East Indies. Nicknamed the "Iron General," Daendels institutes reforms that include the integration of local rulers into the civil service, cleaning up Batavia and giving it a much needed facelift. He razes much of the old city in the process and chooses to run the government from a palace in cool, outlying Buitenzorg on the property of the present palace in Central Bogor.

**1809** — Daendels starts building a new palace for Batavia on Waterloo Square (presently Lapangan Banteng, the "Place of Buffalos"), east of Weltevreden and De Harmonie, a private club. Fortifications in Batavia are strengthened against the increasingly aggressive British naval presence.

**1811** — Napoleon formally annexes the Netherlands. Daendels raises the French flag over Batavia but is recalled from his post as Governor-General. On August 8, a British expeditionary force from Malacca, led by Thomas Stamford Raffles,

Lieutenant-Governor of the British East India Company, invades and finds little resistance from the French and sympathetic support from the Dutch. Within a month, the British control Batavia. Historian, writer, naturalist, humanist, diplomat, as well as conqueror, Raffles embarks on an even more ambitious program of reforms for Batavia and the whole of the East Indies — a progressive, new political, social and economic system.

**1812** — Raffles, with the assistance of American botanist Dr. Thomas Horsfield, begins collecting plant and tree specimens for the expansive garden at the palace in Buitenzorg that lay the groundwork for the world famous Bogor Botanical Gardens. Raffles provides inspiration for the Batavia Society of Arts and Sciences and begins collecting material for his monumental "History of Java". He introduces a land tax system, overhauls the civil service and improves the plight of indigenous peoples.

**1815** — The "Societeit de Harmonie" inaugurates its swank clubhouse. The Java Government Gazetteer describes it as the most elite spot in town if not all Asia, boasting "spacious marble halls with beautiful marble pillars, crystal chandeliers, wall mirrors and bronze".

**1816** — Napoleon's adventures in empire-building ended, the Dutch regain control of their homeland and, over Raffles' objections, Batavia. His reforms barely implemented, Raffles is seen off by scores of important English, Dutch and Indonesian friends on March 23 and sails on to gain greater glory as the founder of Singapore.

**1818** — The Koningsplein ("King's Square"), the vast parkland south of Weltevreden now called Merdeka Square, becomes a training field for the military. Jalan Veteran, at the time called Rijswijk, becomes a "respectable" street for Europeans and local people, and Chinese and Indonesians are forced to relocate their shops as fashionable boutiques spring up along the desirable promenade.

**1821** — Gedung Kesenian, later the City Theatre, is constructed on the site where thespians from the ranks of the British army ranks once gave dramatic performances in a bamboo shed. A major restoration project, begun in 1986, will later return the historic theater to its original function, as a center for the performing arts.

**1822** — An outbreak of cholera claims the lives of 158 people in Batavia and 773 people in the environs. Only the strong survive the inept treatment at the city's hospitals.

**1825** — The five-year Java War begins, led by Indonesian hero Prince Diponegoro. As many as 200,000 Indonesians die during the guerrilla war. As a consequence, the colonial administration tightens control over Central and East Java and implements a system of dual, but far from equal, European and native rule.

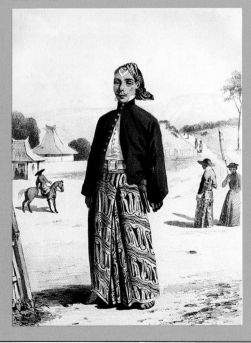

1826 — Scottish entrepreneur Gillian Maclaine, an associate of Raffles, and Thomas Watson, founders of the Maclaine Watson firm in Batavia (the headquarters were later moved to Singapore) introduce the first coastal steamship service to ferry passengers and cargos between Java and Singapore.

1828 — The palace on Lapangan Banteng started by Daendels is completed. Although *het Witte Huis* ("The White House") has been used for many government functions, including its present status as the Ministry of Finance, it never was to serve its intended purpose.

1830 — Johnannes Count van den Bosch is appointed Governor-General of the Netherlands East Indies. He introduces the *Cultuurstelsel*, a stiff land tax on crops, in an effort to encourage the proliferation of export crop plantations. It fuels renewed profitability for the Netherlands and eventually accounts for 30 per cent of the budget of The Hague. But this system of compulsory crop production stirs new anti-Dutch resentment among the Javanese and Sundanese peasant farmers.

1835 — A troop of French opera singers are stranded in Batavia. They give up their arias to become hairdressers and tailors.

1839 — The architecture of the city relinquishes some Dutch colonial influences and takes on wider European expressions. The Emmanuel Church on the Koningsplein is built reflecting the neoclassical architecture of Europe. Soon after, the Roman Catholic Cathedral on Lapangan Banteng adds a Gothic touch to the city.

1857 — Telegraph lines connect Batavia and Buitenzorg for the first time.

1859 — Batavia and Singapore are linked by a revolutionary cable service.

1860 — Edward Douwes Dekker, a Dutch-born colonial official, publishes *Max Havelaar* under the pen name Multatuli. The novel is a scathing indictment of the oppressive Dutch rule in Java that exposes the cynicism, corruption and bankrupt policies of Dutch officials in the colony and champions the plight of the impoverished, exploited peasants. *Max Havelaar* causes a public outcry in the Netherlands that leads to the dismantling of the *Cultuurstelsel*, except for the forced cultivation of coffee which continues until 1917. Slavery is formally abolished. Despite the more liberal policies, the winds of nationalism have begun blowing. (Dekker later becomes the only Westerner honored as a hero of the Indonesian revolution.)

1868 — Construction of the National Museum is completed by the influential Batavian Society of Arts and Sciences.

1869 — The opening of the Suez Canal stimulates the growth in the Dutch Indies of cash-crop exports like cocoa, sugar, palm oil, tobacco, and tea. It also produces an influx of foreign travelers to Batavia lured by adventure books published about the exotic Islands of the East Indies.

1873 — The Batavia to Buitenzorg railway opens.

1877 — Batavia's harbor operations are moved eight kilometers east of Sunda Kelapa, which is too shallow to handle the increasing volume of goods, to the new deep-water port of Tanjung Priok.

1879 — Construction of the Governor-General's palace is completed behind van Braam's "country house" facing the Koningsplein.

1880 — Telephone service is introduced in Batavia.

1900 — Buoyed by new profits and tourism, Batavia once again takes on the look of a "Queen of the East" with well-scrubbed streets, restaurants, neat hotels, shady parks and broad avenues lined by grand houses in such new suburban districts as Gondangdia, Menteng and Tanah Abang. Even the old quarters around the City Hall are cleaned, swept, drained and painted. The simpler, but neat, residential areas, the *kampungs* of Indonesians from other islands and other parts of Java, also start to spring up.

1901 — The Ethical Policy of political and social reforms is introduced by the Dutch with a view towards improving the plight of Indonesians. Expenditures on public health and sanitation projects and education are increased. Steps are taken to decentralize the government from Batavia to the regions and from Dutch hands to Indonesian.

1908 — A group of politically-minded students at Batavia's Stovia Medical School form Budi Utomo ("Pure Endeavor"), the first organization with nationalistic aspirations. Similar organizations begin to bloom throughout the archipelago.

1918 — First meeting of the Volksraad (People's Council), a body composed of elected and appointed Dutch and Indonesian advisors. The council is a belated Dutch attempt to give the Indonesians a bigger voice in government.

1919 — Sarekat Islam, a political and religious organization formed in 1912, attracts 2.5 million members. The rising international Islamic consciousness plays a central role in the burgeoning resistance to colonial rule.

1924 — *Partai Komunis Indonesia,* or PKI, the Indonesian Communist Party, is formed. Concerned about the increasing political activities, the Dutch government begins jailing and exiling some of its political party leaders.

1926 — PKI-instigated revolts occur in Batavia and surrounding areas. The Dutch crush the insurrection and jail thousands, obliterating the PKI.

1927 — A student named Sukarno, the handsome son of a Javanese teacher and his Balinese wife from

*Statues of Indonesia's first president and vice-president, Sukarno, left, and Mohammad Hatta, right, flank the monument that commemorates the 1945 declaration of independence on the grounds of the first president's home off Jalan Proklamasi.*

East Java, rounds up some of his colleagues at the Technical College at Bandung, a mountain town south of Batavia with a tradition as a hotbed of political activity among student intellectuals. He founds a new political party called Perserikatan Nasional Indonesia (PNI) that has the express goal of gaining independence from the Dutch.

**1928** — The All Indonesia Youth Congress is held in Batavia. It adopts a historic resolution unanimously proclaiming three ideals: one Indonesian Fatherland, one Indonesian nation and a single language of unity, Bahasa Indonesia.

**1929** — PNI membership tops 10,000, mostly in Batavia, Bandung and Surabaya. Sukarno is arrested by the Dutch administration for his increasingly anti-colonial, fiery speechmaking. He is convicted on a charge of threatening public order and imprisoned.

**1931** — The Dutch government dissolves the PNI. Sutan Sjahrir and Mohammad Hatta, Indonesians who had been studying at universities in the Netherlands, return and form a new PNI. They become Sukarno's chief rivals in the struggle for leadership of the independence movement.

**1933** — Sukarno is arrested again and exiled on this occasion to Flores.

**1934** — Hatta and Sjahrir are arrested and exiled.

**1936** — The Volksraad approves a petition calling for Indonesian authority within a Dutch-Indonesian union to be arranged over the next decade.

**1937** — The first "city plan" for Batavia is formed with the Koningsplein as its center.

**1940** — As World War II rages, Adolph Hitler invades Holland and the Netherlands government flees to exile in London. All progress toward autonomy for Indonesia ceases. Meanwhile, a 19-year-old Javanese named Suharto enters the military school in Central Java.

**1942** — Having swept through the Philippines, Hong Kong, Malaysia and Singapore, the Japanese overrun much of the East Indies and march into Batavia on March 5. They rename the city Jakarta, portray themselves as liberators of the Indonesian people from Dutch colonialism, then proceed to impose their own harsh form of imperialism and exploitation throughout the archipelago as well as Jakarta.

**1943** — Japan's anti-Western campaign invigorates anti-Dutch sentiment in the islands. An Indonesian military force is trained by the Japanese.

### Independence (from 1945)

**1945** — The Japanese war effort runs out of steam and defeat appears imminent. Indonesian leaders urge the Japanese to declare the islands independent in hopes of heading off a return of Dutch authority. Sukarno delivers his most important speech in the old Volksraad. Standing between the

two huge pillars where the Dutch Governor-Generals once stood, he unwraps his "five precious pearls", the basis for the principles of the national philosophy of Pancasila — nationalism, internationalism, social justice and belief in one God — providing a rallying ideology for the independence movement. Then, on a hot August night in Jakarta the day after Japan surrenders to the Allied Forces, Sukarno and Hatta work feverishly in the home of the Japanese naval liaison officer who is sympathetic to their cause to draft another document. On the morning of August 17, Sukarno reads a proclamation of *merdeka* ("independence") in the garden of his Jakarta home at Jalan Pegansaan Timur 56 and the red-and-white flag of Indonesia is raised for the first time. Sukarno is elected president of the new nation, Hatta vice-president. Jakarta becomes its capital. To the dismay of the Indonesians, the Dutch maintain that they still have sovereignty over the islands and the Allies balk at getting involved in the dispute. Sjahrir becomes prime minister and enters into intense negotiations with the Dutch. But revolutionary tensions mount.

**1946** — Fighting breaks out in parts of Java. Sukarno, Hatta and other important officials secretly depart from Jakarta's Koningsplein railway station for Yogyakarta where they plot strategy against the Dutch. Jakarta reverts to a colonial capital where the Dutch authorities mobilize their military might. The war for independence begins.

**1947** — Negotiations toward a settlement of the Dutch-Indonesian conflict begin on an American cruiser, the USS Renville, in Tanjung Priok harbor.

**1948** — People from other parts of the nation pour into Jakarta. The population burgeons to one million. Resources are overtaxed. Some 700,000 fruit trees of 26 different varieties are leveled in Kebayoran Baru to make room for people. Shantytowns begin to blight the landscape.

**1949** — Pressured by the costs of continuing the war and by international opinion, the Dutch concede defeat and recognize the Independent Republic of the United States of Indonesia, excluding Dutch New Guinea (West Irian). President Sukarno returns triumphantly to Jakarta aboard a freshly-painted Garuda Indonesia Airways plane (that had been a KLM plane the day before) on December 27 and raises the Indonesian Merah-Putih (red-and-white) flag at Merdeka Palace.

**1950** — Jakarta enters a period of physical decline as Sukarno and his colleagues struggle to forge a viable government and a unified nation from the splintered archipelago. Over the next seven years, political infighting sees a series of governments, each with an average life span of eight months. Through this period of "liberal democracy", the charismatic Sukarno hangs on as the new nation's leader in the midst of the turmoil.

**1951** — The communist PKI begins to make a spectacular comeback.

**1952** — Some 30,000 squatter shacks of unregistered "homeless" people are counted in Jakarta.

**1955** — Indonesia holds its first general election. The PNI receives a majority vote. Sukarno hosts the Afro-Asian Conference of non-aligned Third World nations in Bandung that brings such luminaries as Zhou Enlai, Nehru, Nasser, Sihanouk, U Nu and Pham Van Dong to Indonesia.

**1957** — While under detention for reporting about high-level corruption, journalist Mochtar Lubis writes his landmark novel *Twilight in Jakarta*. It describes the dark, chaotic, bleak side of life among the minions of the city. Faced with rebellions in the outer islands and a nation that is falling apart, Sukarno declares martial law and unveils his more authoritarian policy of "Guided Democracy".

**1959** — The development of Jakarta becomes part of Sukarno's "lighthouse" policy designed to make Indonesia the center of the emerging Third World nations. But economic chaos sets in instead as the rupiah is devalued by 75 per cent.

**1960** — Rebuffed on his proposed budget, Sukarno dissolves Parliament. He argues for an unwieldy doctrine called Nasakom, a government that unifies the nationalism represented by the PNI, the Islam of other powerful political parties and the PKI's Marxism. Meanwhile, the army tries to restrict the increasing activities of the PKI.

**1961** — Indonesia enters a period of hyperinflation of about 100 per cent annually and increasing radicalism. Despite serious economic problems, Sukarno lays the cornerstone for Monas, the national monument, in the middle of the 100 hectare park on the former Koningsplein. The flame atop the great obelisk reflects the inextinguishable fighting spirit of Indonesian revolutionaries. Sukarno also lavishes money on extravagant building projects and monuments while millions in the country languish in poverty.

**1962** — After a series of military skirmishes, commanded by Major-General Suharto, the Dutch agree to transfer sovereignty of West Irian to Indonesia. Sukarno builds the Senayan Sports Stadium with Russian assistance and Jakarta hosts the fourth Asian Games.

**1963** — Sukarno severs relations with the Federation of Malaysia, (comprised of the former British colonies of Malaya, Singapore, Sabah and Sarawak) and invades the East Malaysian states in northern Borneo. In Jakarta, Communist thugs burn the British embassy and the Cricket Club and attack the embassy of Malaysia. The PKI aligns itself with

China against the Soviet Union and party membership exceeds 2 million, making it the largest Communist party outside the Communist block. Suharto is put in charge of Kostrad, the Army Strategic Reserve Command. Meanwhile, Jakarta hosts the "Games for the New Emerging Forces" of the Third World. The international exposure prompts the construction of new roads, the Hotel Indonesia and Sarinah's department store.

**1965** — As "confrontation" continues in the Borneo jungles, Indonesia withdraws from the United Nations when Malaysia is accorded a Security Council seat. China's premier, Zhou Enlai, visits Jakarta and seals an alliance with Indonesia. With anti-Western sentiment increasing, the American Peace Corps is expelled from Indonesia. Inflation reaches 500 per cent.

Inspired by their growing might and with support of some military factions, a PKI faction called GESTAPU, the "September 30 movement", attempts to overthrow the government. Six senior army generals and an officer are abducted from their homes in Jakarta on the night of September 30, then brutally murdered. Their bodies are then brutally mutilated by youth members and thrown in *Lubang Buaya*, "crocodile hole".

Suharto quickly assumes command of the army and restores order. The attempted coup collapses in confusion. In anti-communist reprisals, hundreds of thousands throughout the archipelago are believed killed during the following months and thousands more imprisoned. As the PKI is crushed, order returns to the capital and the new leaders approve a Master Plan for the Special Territory of Jakarta (DKI) detailing its development over the next 20 years. The plan calls for a balanced expansion within a 15 kilometer radius of Monas.

**1966** — Suharto abandons confrontation with Malaysia, returns Indonesia to the UN and looks to the West for aid in rebuilding the country. Ali Sadikin is appointed governor of Jakarta. He rehabilitates its rutted roads, rundown transportation system and shabby buildings. *Becaks* are banned from the main roads. The city's population reaches 4.5 million. Jakarta is officially designated the legal capital of the Republic of Indonesia.

**1967** — Sukarno is relieved of remaining powers and, put under house arrest by a reformed consultative assembly. Suharto is appointed acting President and consolidates his "New Order" government. Ties with China are severed and its embassy in Jakarta's Glodok district is shut down.

Replacing the themes of revolution and nationalism that had been his predecessor's preoccupation, Suharto appoints a group of California-trained technocrats known as the "Berkeley mafia" to rebuild the nation's shattered economy. Inflation is slashed 100 per cent. Governor Sadikin builds more schools in one year than were built during the previous 16 years. Despite Muslim prohibition against gambling, he establishes lotteries and casinos in the city to help finance Jakarta's redevelopment. Indonesia joins Malaysia, Singapore, Thailand and the Philippines in the formation of the Association of Southeast Asian Nations (ASEAN) which focuses on regional economic cooperation and development. Jakarta is later selected as the site of ASEAN's headquarters.

**1968** — Suharto is officially confirmed as President of the Republic. In contrast to Sukarno's flamboyant manner, Suharto maintains a low profile. Rather than move to the presidential palace, he stays put in his more modest home in Menteng.

**1969** — World Bank funds assist in the Kampung Improvement Projects and Jakarta's "urban villages" are paved, sanitation and sewage upgraded and more schools and medical facilities established. Repelita I, the first five-year development plan, is announced. Election laws establish a Parliament (DPR) and People's Consultative Assembly (MPR) in Jakarta. West Irian, now Irian Jaya, is incorporated into Indonesia as its 26th province.

**1970** — Sukarno dies. The nation mourns.

**1972** — Restoration of the historical buildings of Old Batavia begins, notwithstanding the bitter memories of the colonial era.

**1973** — The world energy crisis sparks major increases in oil prices improving the economic outlook for Indonesia, the region's major oil producer and exporter.

**1975** — Western colonialism in the archipelago ends when Portugal pulls out of East Timor. Fearing a leftist takeover there, Indonesia sends in troops and in the following year integrates East Timor into Indonesia as its 27th province.

**1977** — Spiraling oil prices fuel miracle economic growth rates averaging 7.6 per cent annually. With petroleum accounting for 70 per cent of the nation's earnings, concerned planners increase efforts to diversify the country's economic foundation. But massive unemployment and poverty continue to plague the whole archipelago.

**1980** — Development of Jakarta accelerates but so do its problems as improvement in infrastructure fails to keep pace with its explosive growth. The population of the city nears 6 million.

**1985** — The U.S.$300 million Soekarno-Hatta International Airport opens in Cengkareng, west of Jakarta. Dunia Fantasie ("Fantasy World") theme park opens in the Ancol Dreamland amusement complex. The old Harmonie Club, long neglected, is demolished to improve traffic flow.

Contrary to popular awareness, Jakarta is one of the earliest settled capitals in Asia. Large caches of tools, pottery and ceramics that date back to Neolithic times have been unearthed in many parts of the city.

The most notable find was a boulder carved with the Wenggi characters used by the Pallava dynasty of Conjeveram in south India. The fifth century A.D. inscriptions tell of the Hindu state of Taruma, governed by a king named Purnawarman who built a canal through the flat coastal plain to relieve flooding. Heavy rains still cause problems, however.

in Sumatra. The next Hindu dynasty to emerge in the vicinity was that of the Sunda kingdom ruled from Pajajaran, south of modern Bogor, which lasted until the coming of the Portuguese in the 16th century.

The stone with Purnawarman's inscriptions, known as the *Prasasti Tugu*, is kept in the National Museum, along with other relics of the capital's earliest settlement, and a replica is on exhibit in the Jakarta Museum in the

Historians believe that canal is the Citarum or Tarum River (the prefix *ci* means river) which today runs from the Jatiluhur reservoir southeast of the city to the Java Sea. The seat of Purnawarman's kingdom is believed to have been located east of Jakarta in the town of Bekasi, the site of other antiquities.

At that early time, Tarumanegara apparently already had well-established trade ties with China. In the seventh century, it fell to the Buddhist Srivijaya empire, believed to be based near the present day city of Palembang

*Exquisitely-carved Balinese wood works of Garuda and Vishnu and a wooden screen inlaid with hand-tooled leather panels of* wayang kulit *figures are among the elaborate displayed art in the Istana Merdeka, Independence Palace.*

restored "Old Batavia" district of Taman Fatahillah. The historic inscription takes its name from the atmospheric old part of the city where it was discovered.

Tugu is the kind of place you might never stumble upon if you were not conscientiously looking for it, engulfed as it is by the civil service housing estates and noisome landfills of northeast Jakarta. But then much of the fascination of Jakarta lies in such inconspicuous nooks and crannies.

Tugu nestles in a cool copse of coconut palms and mango trees near the city's teeming industrial hub, Tanjung Priok, where multitudes live and work in the shadow of the monolithic silos of the Bogasari Flour mills. Yet, the dignified air of antiquity cushions Tugu from the surrounding clamor.

A simple stucco church built by Portuguese settlers in 1744 stands on a plot studded with

European names like Montaga and Seymons. In 1522, Portugal became the first Western country to establish a foothold in the Indonesian archipelago. The district of Tugu thus ushers the visitor into the first well-documented era of the city's history.

The Portuguese presence was brief but influential. Indonesian words like *bola*, for ball, *bendera*, for flag, *mentaga*, for butter, and even *merdeka*, the word for independence, are all derived from the Portuguese.

In Tugu, the Portuguese influence is particularly evident. A few of the residents that still live there are descended from the *mardijkers*, Portuguese colonial subjects of Malay and Indian origin who were captured and then freed by the Dutch after they accepted conversion to Christianity.

The Quiko family, caretakers of the church, trace their lineage to those times. The matriarch of the family lives next door in a boxy wooden house decorated with crucifixes and ceramics painted with pictures of saints. Her son, Fernando, tries to keep Tugu's ancient heritage intact as chairman of the community's historical and cultural committee.

"Jakarta was a jewel of a city when our ancestors first came to Tugu," Fernando explains with pride. "Couples used to spend romantic evenings floating down the Ciliwung River in gondolas."

Unfortunately, the Ciliwung River has long since become a fetid catch-all for the city's refuse. "As the boats plied the river, lovers could hear the strains of the *keroncong* being played along the banks" added Fernando.

*Keroncong* music, with its melancholy melodies of Moorish and Middle Eastern origin, is Tugu's most enduring contribution to Indonesian culture. Played by small orchestras of

string instruments that resemble ukeleles and mandolins, Indonesia's modern-day composers and performers still invoke its moods in contemporary songs that echo Jakarta's timeless mystery and magic.

When the Portuguese arrived, economic activity was focused on Sunda Kelapa, northwest of Tugu and Tanjung Priok, the harbor that by then was a bustling hub of the Sundanese kingdom of Pajajaran. Tome Pirés, who visited in 1512, described Sunda Kelapa as the finest harbor in Java in his classic portrait of the Far East, *Suma Oriental*.

Today, *pinisi* schooners of the Bugis still dock at Sunda Kelapa, just behind the city's

*Another wide-angle view of the Istana Merdeka's interior reveals more arts and crafts: the paneled* wayang kulit *screen, doric columns, marble floors, an expansive carpet and an ornate table in the shape of a coach.*

pungent, fly-infested fish market, the *Pasar Ikan*. A ticket from the port authority buys today's explorers passage into another age. It is one of Jakarta's most enthralling sites. Except for the lorries, Sunda Kelapa looks much the same as it must have five centuries ago, barefoot porters load and unload merchandise from the handsome hand-made wooden schooners. They are built on the idyllic southwestern beaches of the island of

Museum were later erected by the Dutch on the foundations of the Kasteel.

Despite the alliance between the Portuguese and the king of Sunda, Demak's Muslim leader, Fatahillah, scored a pair of victories and moved into Kelapa. On June 22, 1527, the day still celebrated as the city's birthday, Fatahillah renamed it Jayakarta, usually translated as "Glorious Victory" or "Perfect Triumph". The name of a vassal of Demak,

Sulawesi, northeast of Java, by the archipelago's seafaring Bugis people.

Still, Sunda Kelapa was overshadowed in Pirés time by Banten, also known as Bantam, on the nub of land to the northwest that sailors called Java Head. Banten is a worthwhile sidetrip for history and archaeology buffs because some of its landmarks have been restored, including an impressive Grand Mosque. In addition, the walls of fortresses like the Dutch-built Speelwijk have been excavated from centuries of silt.

In 1525, the powerful East Java kingdom of Demak conquered Banten and used it to stage an assault on Sunda and its fine harbor. Fearing the growing might of Demak, the king of Sunda had signed a friendship treaty with Portugal in 1522 that resulted in the construction of Kasteel Jakarta at Kelapa. The old fortress walls in the vicinity of the Bahari

Banten's third Muslim leader Prince Jayawikarta, has given rise to an alternative theory of the historic origin of the city's name.

But it was the Dutch, who had already begun moving into the lucrative spice trade in the Moluccas islands east of Java, that laid the groundwork for Jakarta's rise as the capital of the archipelago. Frustrated by Javanese leaders and rival European fleets in his plans to use Banten as the base for Dutch mercantile expansion in the islands, Jan Pieterszoon Coen turned his attention to Jayakarta, or Jacatra as it was also known. In 1619, he attacked Jayakarta, drove out British forces that were stationed there and renamed his new base

*High-tech has come to Jakarta with the help of Prof. Dr. B.J. Habibie, Minister for Research and Technology (left), who has developed a growing aircraft industry manned by highly-skilled technicians (above).*

59

Batavia in honor of an ancient Germanic tribe that were the forefathers of the Dutch.

Coen's employer was the mighty Dutch East India Company, also known as the VOC or Jan Compagnie. His first move as the founding Governor-General of the colony was to transfer all the VOC's money and merchandise from Banten to Batavia, the VOC's new headquarters. That accomplished, Coen transformed Batavia into a carbon copy of a Dutch coastal town and, more significantly, into one of the world's busiest, richest and most important capital cities for entrepreneurs of the time. It became the nerve center of a far-flung colonial empire that included not only the Netherlands East Indies (which eventually included most of modern Indonesia), but stretched all the way from Ceylon to Japan.

The VOC's fleet filled Batavia's sprawling warehouses with cloves, mace and nutmegs, pepper and sandalwood. In exchange for these desirable commodities, Batavia's banks filled up with silver *reals* and gold.

This phase of Jakarta's history still endures in the weathered old godowns, buildings and residences around Sunda Kelapa and Kota, the city's Chinatown area. The present Indonesian administration, wisely choosing to ignore critics who want to bury all evidence of the colonial past, has restored some of the significant buildings of that era.

Most prominent is the *Balai Kota*, the old City Hall on the tiled square now called Taman Fatahillah. It was completed in 1710 on the site of earlier buildings and served as the administrative quarters for both the VOC and the Batavia government.

In its halls, self-righteous officials passed judgment on fellow countrymen, as well as Indonesians, who broke Dutch laws, then imprisoned them in the filthy "water prison" under the entrance steps or in crowded dungeons in its depths. The square was the site of public floggings and other barbaric punishments. Executions by hanging, impalement or by a kind of guillotine were also held there while the nattily-dressed Dutch overlords and their retinues looked on with aloof interest from the portico and windows.

The Balai Kota now houses the collections of the Jakarta Museum. Other classical buildings in the area, like the Museum of Fine Arts,

*The statue of an elephant that stands in front of the neoclassical facade of the National Museum was a gift presented by King Chulalongkorn of Siam in 1871, three years after the neoclassical museum building was completed.*

formerly the Palace of Justice, and the quaint Dutch building that contains the superb Wayang puppet collection, were built much later, in the years 1870 and 1912 respectively.

Not far from the square near the Chicken-market bridge over the Kali Besar, are various godowns and corn warehouses and mosques, Chinese temples and churches also date from the early Dutch colonial era. Fortress walls, like those near the Bahari Museum, formed

part of the Bastion Culemborg completed around 1645. The museum itself is in a godown built in 1652. The *Gereja Sion*, also known as the Portuguese Church Outside the Walls, behind the Kota railway station on Jalan Pangeran Jayakarta, dates back to 1695. The Tokoh Merah or "Red Shop" and Chartered Bank building further down the Kali Besar canal from the Chickenmarket Bridge were built early in the 18th century.

In sharp contrast, to the east of the old Sunda Kelapa port today is the popular Taman Impian Jaya Ancol complex, an expansive "dreamland", as its name translates, which the Indonesian government has developed into an

*Ornate tombstones of Dutch aristocracy (above and right) are found at Jakarta's oldest church, Gereja Sion; old and new photographs reveal little change in Batavia bastion walls (following pages) that still stand near the Fish Market.*

impressive recreation area and theme park over the past two decades.

Old Batavia occupied a relatively compact area at first. But it rapidly expanded beyond the confining walls that once protected the old administrative enclave — out of necessity as much as anything. The Dutch neglected to provide a basic infrastructure including proper sanitation and health facilities and the once pleasant city quickly contracted a severe case of urban rot. Conditions were so bad that epidemics swept through the frequently flooded, unhealthy streets of Batavia and, perhaps fittingly, even claimed the life of Governor-General Dirk van Cloon in 1735.

Officials and their families fled to cleaner, cooler rural areas outside the walls. One of the finest country houses of that time, built by an upwardly mobile Governor-General-to-be, Reinier de Klerk in 1760, is now incongruously wedged in among the shophouses that sprang up on Jalan Gajah Madah in the intervening years. The once grand mansion now houses the National Archives.

Otherwise, the alternating rows of tawdry storefronts and newer blocks along both sides of the wide avenues that are split by the dank canal once called Molenvliet house all manner of mundane establishments, from greasy motorcycle repair shops and clean, air-conditioned bakeries to cavernous Chinese restaurants and massage emporiums with alluring names like Dusit Thani.

One of the first efforts to clean up the city and its image was begun by Governor-General Herman Willem Daendels (1808-1811). He is responsible for much of the layout of the inner city that has persisted into the present. He tore down decrepit old buildings and shifted some of the military and administrative operations to new quarters built on the *Weltevreden*, southeast of the city.

Part of that area, now called Gambir, encompassed Lapangan Banteng, the square standing in front of the Hotel Borobudur Intercontinental. The stately buildings there that presently house the Department of Finance and Supreme Court were begun by Daendels. The startling sculpture of a man symbolically breaking his chains in the center of the square is a relic of the latter-day building frenzy of President Sukarno.

Daendels' reign was interrupted by political events in Europe that enabled the British to take over Batavia in 1811. The British appointed a bright, progressive young man as Governor-General, Thomas Stamford Raffles, who later went on to greater glory and a knighthood as the founder of Singapore.

In his monumental *History of Java*, Raffles blamed Batavia's decay on Dutch mismanagement. "The buildings ... are admirably adapted to keep out the fresh air and to retain that which is putrid or noxious," he wrote. He recommended replacing old structures with practical housing and buildings more suited to the humid tropical climate.

generated pestilential malaria, which were transported by the land-wind even to the roads." But by the 1850s, Crawfurd reported that Daendels, Raffles and their successors had filled up the canals, thereby restoring the natural currents and that Batavia was "no more unhealthy than any other tropical city similarly situated."

The new Batavia that developed in the wake of Daendels' and Raffles' improvements was

But before Raffles could implement many reforms, the Dutch returned in 1816. Before he left, the harsh realities of life in Batavia claimed the life of Raffles' beloved first wife, Olivia Miriamme. She is buried under a marked tombstone in the Taman Prasasti on Jalan Tanah Abang I.

Malaria and cholera were the city's major scourges. John Crawfurd, another of the reform-minded British leaders, blamed Jakarta's reputation and realities on the impractical Dutch in his *Descriptive Dictionary of the Indian Islands and Adjacent Countries*: "The Dutch, unmindful of a difference of some 45 degrees of latitude, determined on having a town after the model of those of the Netherlands, within six degrees of the equator and on the level of the sea. The river spread over the town in many handsome canals, lost its current, deposited its copious sediment, and

anchored by the Koningsplein, or King's Square, laid out in 1818. Modern Jakarta revolves in perpetual motion around this dramatic one square kilometer park, now called Medan Merdeka ("Freedom Field") or Monas, after the Monumen Nasional (National Monument). The 137-meter tall marble monument resembles the Washington Monument in the capital city of the United States, except for it pedestal base and a 14.5 meter bronze flame coated with 32 kilograms of pure gold at the top. Monas was another of Sukarno's inspirations completed in 1961. Sukarno's original independence manuscript is exhibited inside in the Hall of Silence, removed from the roar of the legions of rusting green and red three-wheeled Bajaj (Indonesian's call them *bajies*) that buzz constantly on the wide avenues that crisscross the square.

The Dutch were responsible for building

some of the neoclassical structures with Grecian porticos and pillars that border Medan Merdeka. Most notable are the Emmanuel Church, which was opened in 1839 on the eastern flank; the neoclassical National Museum on the west that was completed in 1868 (and is fronted by a bronze elephant presented by the king of Siam in 1871); and the Merdeka (Freedom) Palace, built in 1879, on the north. The Dutch dedicated the palace

The courtyard in front of the palace was the scene of a happier occasion on the morning of December 27, 1949. That was the day the Dutch flag was lowered and the red-and-white banner of Indonesia raised in its place to the patriotic cries of "*Merdeka! Merdeka!* (Freedom, Freedom)" from huge crowds, four years after Sukarno had proclaimed independence in August 9, 1945. That ceremony is reenacted on Independence Day each year as 27 pairs of

to the newlywed King William III.

Since then, Dutch Governor-Generals, Japanese generals and Indonesian presidents have made use of the building. But only the Japanese commanders and President Suharto have actually lived in the building. Sukarno used to hold lavish parties in the gardens where peacocks strutted. The gardens separate Merdeka Palace from the State Palace, built at the end of the 18th century, with a regal facade facing the bustling commercial avenues of Jalan Veteran. A mirror, cracked by a bullet hole, hangs on one wall in the Credential Hall of Merdeka Palace, a reminder of an attempt on Sukarno's life in the 1960s.

*Music lovers crowd cassette stores like Duta Suara where they eagerly sample the latest sounds before making their choice (above). The Welcome Statue (right), is appropriately located in a Menteng traffic circle that is ringed with luxury hotels.*

boys and girls, representing each of Indonesia's provinces, dress in pure white, goose-step towards the flag pole and raise a replica of the original flag to flutter in front of the stately and graceful palace.

Another striking landmark of Medan Merdeka is the austere Istiqlal Mosque on the northeast corner, one of Asia's largest places of Islamic worship. Construction of the mosque begun by Sukarno was not completed until after his death. It is located across from the spires of a 20th century Gothic Roman Catholic cathedral, a proximity that is indicative of the very healthy religious tolerance that is found throughout Indonesia.

South of Monas is Menteng, with its corpulent banyans and graceful homes, which sprang up early this century. The style of many of the older homes is exemplary of the style of Dutch *de Stijl* architecture.

67

**The striking figure of a man** breaking his chains dominates Lapangan Banteng, the square in front of the Borobudur Intercontinental. The monument is one of Jakarta's most familiar landmarks, a symbol of the liberation of Irian Jaya.

# City of Monuments

The founding father and first president of the Republic of Indonesia, Sukarno, once said, "Great nations honor their heroes."

Never one to mince words and discard them, Sukarno punctuated Jakarta with a legion of conspicuous monuments. He hoped they would help Indonesians cultivate pride in themselves, their nation and the individuals, concepts and events which shaped the modern Republic.

The most spectacular and obvious of them all, of course, is Monas, the white obelisk in Medan Merdeka. "We Indonesians call it paku jagat, the 'axis of the world.' That tells you exactly how important this creation is to us," a city government official says. "Our capital is much more European than other Asian cities with regard to the number of statues that have been erected throughout the city."

Covered with imported Italian marble, because the huge quarries in nearby Bandung and in Lampung in South Sumatra had yet to be discovered when it was built, the 137-meter Monas tower is crowned with a gold flame. It is a magnet for Indonesian visitors to the city from all parts of the sprawling archipelago as well as for foreign travelers. "Sukarno's drive for independence is immortalized in Jakarta's monuments. If you study Monas closely, you will find the date of our independence, 8/17/45, used in its measurements," the official explains.

Monas and other statues are so well-known in Jakarta, they are often the landmarks used to provide directions to taxi drivers and chauffeurs. As such, some of them have earned irreverent nicknames, particularly among expatriates who are ignorant of the local mythology and national heroes.

On Jalan Sudirman, for instance, the amazing musculature of the "Pizza Man" also known as "Hot Hands Harry", supports a flaming plate high above his straining body. This statue, officially called Patung Pemuda or Youth Statue, represents the spirit and drive of the young in the development of the country. However, even many Jakartans find the grimace on the face of the statue, donated by Pertamina State Oil Company, a bit humorous.

More effective is the startling statue in Lapangan Banteng (in front of Hotel Borobudur Intercontinental), sometimes referred to as the "Great Hulk". It commemorates Indonesia's military and political triumph in winning sovereignty over the easternmost province of Irian Jaya in 1963, freeing it from Dutch control.

Local pundits once joked that the statue's contorted face meant it was shouting "kosong", (empty), after glimpsing the condition of the bank vaults in the national treasury behind it! Indonesia faced grave financial difficulties in the early 1960s when it was built which prompted the quip.

On Jalan Gatot Subroto, where it intersects with Pancoran, is the "7-Up" man, so-called either because its pedestal is reminiscent of the soft drink logo or because of the statue's strong extended arm. Located in front of the Indonesian Air Force headquarters, the statue is officially named Dirgantara or "Father of the Heavens". (It is not, as is so often mistaken, Hanuman, the heroic monkey god of Indonesia's epic Ramayana legend.)

Interestingly, a Russian Mig fighter jet initially "flew" at the tip of the statue's finger. But when relations with the Soviet Union soured, Sukarno's pragmatism and good taste prevailed. The aircraft ornament was vanquished.

However, the Soviet influence that encompassed Jakarta in the 1950s and early 1960s is still apparent in the neo-realistic style and political themes of Dirgantara and other monuments. The Farmers' Statue, Patung Tani, in the traffic circle in front of the Aryaduta Hyatt Hotel, for instance, was crafted by two Soviet artists, Matvei Manizer and his son, Otto, whom Sukarno met during a trip to Russia. It depicts a young woman acknowledging the decision of her husband, the "ideal man" of the state, to leave home for the revolution.

Manizer's statues can be seen throughout Moscow and the Patung Tani was a gift from the Soviet Union. In fact, it caused a public flap in recent years because of its "communist" implications. One small group lobbied for ridding the city of the statue, but never obtained enough public support for its cause. It remains, in its prominent location, one of the city's best sculpted statues.

The list goes on in a sculptural spectrum ranging from Balinese classical to modern Henry Moore-like expressions. Perhaps the most recognizable work for foreign visitors is the Selamat Datang or "Welcome Statue" in the traffic circle bordered by the Jakarta Mandarin, Hotel Indonesia and British Embassy.

The bronze statue of a happy couple, vigorously waving at the traffic jams of Jalan M.H. Thamrin, was completed in 1961. It was executed by Henk Ngantung, an artist who was also deputy governor of Jakarta at the time, and a team of eight Indonesian sculptors from Karangwuni, Yogyakarta. The figure weighs five-and-a-half tons and stands above a pond with fountains on a pedestal ten meters high.

A considerably scaled down version of the statue was used for the filming of "The Year of Living Dangerously," starring Australian hearthrob Mel Gibson. The movie has made the statue an international landmark, although it has never been screened in Jakarta's cinemas. Because of the sensitive subject matter of the movie, the film version of the statue was erected in the Muslim quarter of Manila, the location in which the movie was shot.

Despite the neighborhood's posh trappings, one of Jakarta's most bizarre attractions unfolds each night in Menteng, under the banyans, in the dark tributaries of Jalan Latuharhary. This is the road that runs parallel to the railroad tracks and Ciliwung River, around Taman Lawang, and under the bridge near the Chinese restaurants, steak houses and food stalls of Jalan Blora. There, most any night, Jakarta's *bancis* congregate. Dressed to the nines, these "ladies" of the evening expose lacy lingerie, or the lack of same, in scenes reminiscent of a Fellini film.

Look more closely. You will find that many of the "girls" have a tell-tale five o'clock shadow or unusually masculine voices. *Bancis* — also called *waria*—are Jakarta's legion of transvestites. But when traveling through the district, it is advisable to do so in a car. Keep the windows rolled up as the *bancis* can

become quite aggressive if you show even a mild interest in sampling their sexual wares.

The *banci* phenomenon neither raises the eyebrows nor the hackles of Indonesians. In fact, former Jakarta Governor Ali Sadikin arranged social clubs and beauty contests. *Banci* are an offshoot of ancient social systems common in many parts of Asia in which young women were shielded from society until marriage and such pseudo-women as *bancis* became proxies in the dramatic arts, the court and other facets of life.

Just east of Menteng is Jakarta's most celebrated restaurant. The Oasis on Jalan Raden Saleh is beautifully established in what

*One of Asia's best kept secrets is Jakarta's lively nightlife. People like to party long into early morning under the strobe lights at the venerable Tanamur Disco (**left**) and at the Jaya Pub (**above**), a popular club where jazz entertains the crowd.*

**Batik king Iwan Tirta** uses the traditional *canting* pipe to apply hot wax to an intricate pattern drawn in fabric. Tirta and other Indonesian designers have rejuvenated the art with contemporary designs.

# Ancient Art, Modern Fashion

American President Ronald Reagan and First Lady Nancy Reagan caused a minor sensation when they appeared at a dinner party on the Indonesian isle of Bali during an official visit in 1986. The First Couple were swathed in batik of cheerfully colorful design.

President Reagan's traditional long-sleeved, hip-covering formal shirt, a gift from President Suharto, was emblazoned with huge presidential seals in white, mustard and brown. Mrs. Reagan was stunning in a bright red silk batik gown patterned with blue butterflies and lilies. Their outfits, as well as many of those worn by the 140 guests, were the handiwork of Jakarta's Iwan Tirta, widely-recognized as Indonesia's leading batik designer.

Once used exclusively to decorate the clothing of the Javanese aristocracy in ancient times, batik fabrics are now incorporated in contemporary fashion world-wide thanks largely to the Iwan's efforts. His designs, modeled by dazzling Indonesian beauties, have been applauded at shows in Paris and other fashion capitals. Fashion conscious women including Queen Elizabeth II, Jihan Sadat and Imelda Marcos have also worn Tirta's originals.

Batik is the name of a process (rather than the name of a type of fabric or weaving) used in applying patterns to cloth. In fact, the word batik is derived from the Javanese ntik, meaning to make dots.

The process is labor intensive; molten wax is applied with a small, pointed copper pipe with a wooden handle called a canting, then the material is dipped into a dye and the portion of the fabric that is not covered with wax absorbs the color. The material is dipped in boiling water to soften the wax so it can be scraped off. In order to obtain a desired pattern and color scheme, the process may be repeated numerous times on a single bolt of cloth.

Iwan's research has dated the origins of the tedious techniques back at least to the 16th century when the nobles of Java wanted to wear something more decorative and expensive than the handwoven cloth of the time.

"Batik was to the Javanese aristocrats what tartan was to the Scots. It determined their rank and even popularity in royal circles," says Iwan. A two-and-a-half meter length of the finest, hand-drawn batik often took up to six months to finish.

Besides its social function, batik has acquired some fabled properties over the years. It has been said to improve a person's health, avert impending disasters, even calm angry volcanos. When the powerful goddess of the South Seas, Ratu Kidul, turns the waters of the Indian Ocean into a tumultuous storm of waves, bolts of batik are placed on a small raft as an offering to placate the sea goddess' short-fused supernatural wrath.

As the popularity of batik and its designs spread in the early 19th century, the cap, a copper stamp composed of hundreds of small wires used to apply wax in repetitive designs, provided a fast, low-cost alternative to hand-drawing. But, at least, the process used was still batik. In the early 1960s, however, machine screen printing of textile with designs permitted mass production and export. That gave batik a bad name.

"People began thinking of batik as cheap cloth because of the machine-made prints flooding the markets. These are not batik. It is the wax process that gives it the right to be called batik," Iwan says, noting that hand-made batik has a depth and richness that is absent in machine prints. His own creations command prices of Rp50,000 and up for men's shirts to Rp2 million or more for an original gown.

It is that rich, alluring quality that is immediately apparent when one walks into Iwan's headquarters and boutique at Jalan Panarukan 25 (Tel. 337–244) in Jakarta's exclusive old colonial Menteng quarter. Geometric shapes of indigo and dark brown (the traditional batik colors of dignity) from Central Java mix with bright floral patterns with the Chinese influence of Java's north coast. Stylish renderings of archaic art patterns from the Asmat tribe of Irian Jaya, the Dyaks of Kalimantan and others are side-by-side on racks of dresses, shirts and rolls of fabric with patterns of Japanese cherry blossoms, swirling art nouveau motifs and other contemporary designs in electric colors.

Undoubtedly, the kaleidoscope of patterns reflect Tirta's own personality. He is one of the most colorful and familiar characters of Jakarta's arts and social scene; a witty, articulate man who enjoys life in Indonesia's bustling capital. "I found my niche here," he says.

Oddly enough, Iwan launched his career headed in a direction far from the world of fashion. In the 1960s, he graduated with honors from Yale Law School and taught international law at Cornell and the University of California in Berkeley. Considered a rising young political star, he returned to Indonesia. While studying traditional arts in the royal courts of Central Java, he discovered that he was more interested in batik and its design potential than politics. He opened a batik factory in the early 1970s.

"I said goodbye to everything," Iwan said in an interview with the Los Angeles Times. But it was a goodbye without regrets. His breezy, new approach to what was once considered a tired technique was an immediate success. Other stores began to emulate many of Iwan's innovations. Today, his influence is readily apparent in the cool, contemporary lines available from competitors like Batik Danar Hadi, and the nation's largest manufacturer, Batik Keris.

was one of Jakarta's most fabled mansions. Modern lore has it that the building was the home of a Dutch baron who was arrested and jailed in 1940 for allegedly collaborating with the Nazis. When the Japanese were about to invade the city, the home supposedly served as a hideout for the Dutch Governor-General. Whether such tales are true, however, has no bearing on the fact that the Oasis remains one of the most delightful places in the city to enjoy dinner.

To the southeast of the Oasis there were once such other Dutch suburbs as Jatinegara and Meester Cornelis. No longer the exclusive enclaves that they were early this century, these areas have been overwhelmed by crowded *kampungs* and middle-class residential and commercial developments.

Jakarta's expansion directly south of Menteng brings the chronology of the city's development up to the middle of the 20th century. Paramita Abdurachman, a historian with one of Indonesia's research institutes, says that Menteng was exclusively Dutch and that everything to the south was still rural until as recently as the 1950s.

"It wasn't until after World War II that everything began to be built up," she says. "People began moving this way because it was cooler. There was nothing between Kebayoran Baru and the Hotel Indonesia back then and you could feel the difference in temperature in the evenings."

Paramita now lives near chaotic Blok M in Kebayoran Baru, a spot she said was once lush with orchards of Kemang trees. A neighboring district has retained the name Kemang, but is now lush with enormous new mansions for Indonesia's monied elite. "I haven't seen a Kemang tree for a long time. I guess they've all been cut down to make room for people."

Blok M, contrary to its name which makes it sound like a science fiction designation for some distant part of the galaxy, is the southern shopping and transport nexus of the city. Its sidewalks are choked with commuters in transit and peddlers selling everything from cheap plastic imitations of Porsche sunglasses to potent aphrodisiacs. There are also some fine restaurants, pubs and Japanese nightclubs in the innermost recesses of Blok M.

The areas between Menteng and Kebayoran

*National and international sports events including the Asian Games have been held at the enormous Senayan Stadium, adjacent to the Jakarta Hilton. The complex, opened in 1962, accommodates crowds of up to 120,000.*

74

Baru began building up during Sukarno's latter years and during President Suharto's present administration. Sukarno relied greatly on financial and technical assistance and consultation from the Soviet Union in the early Sixties. That connection is readily apparent in the austere and utilitarian architecture of some of the drab concrete buildings.

Most evident is the massive Senayan Stadium and Sports complex, behind the Jakarta

sculptures and batik table cloths, pillow cases and more.

The Sukarno years are also recalled in the L-shaped Hotel Indonesia, built in the early sixties to impress visitors to the Asian Games. Once Jakarta's premier hotel, Sheraton took over the management for a time but dropped out. Since then the "Ha-Ee", as taxi drivers and Jakartans fondly call it, has been overshadowed by new hotels like the white-washed

Hilton Hotel, built for the Asian Games of 1962. The streets of the stadium's residential complex for visiting athletes are named after sports like Jalan Bulutangkis for badminton, the sport at which Indonesians excel. (Indonesia regularly wins the world championships.) Crowds of up to 120,000 listened, transfixed, to Sukarno's fiery speeches at mass rallies which were held in the stadium in the early 1960s. Now the crowds cheer soccer matches and track and field events.

Another relic of the Sukarno era is the Sarinah Department Store, a monolithic square slab of concrete that now looks out of place amid the glossy glass and metal towers of Jalan Thamrin. Despite its uninviting appearance, the store's third and fourth floors are crammed with an excellent variety of Indonesian handicrafts and clothes, from Balinese carvings and paintings to silver jewelry and

Jakarta Mandarin across the street. It is now primarily a venue for visiting delegates to the steady stream of international conferences and seminars that are held in the capital.

Today, most of the Gatot Subroto/Thamrin/ Kuningan rectangle (the "Ha-Ee" is the northwest corner) is filled with posh hotels, office towers and country clubs. There are glitzy discos and elegant dining places. Even the Kentucky Fried Chicken outlets are clean, modern and expensive. Yet, smack in the middle of it all are a few *kampungs*.

Today's Jakarta sprawls south of Blok M and Kebayoran Baru with hardly a break in development and traffic between it and Bogor,

*President Ronald Reagan's likeness appeared in unlikely places in the capital (**left**) during his 1986 visit to Indonesia. Such images, and billboards with patriotic themes and messages (**above**) are a colorful part of the city landscape.*

once considered a distant town, and now accessible in 40 minutes via the Jagowari Toll Road. Years ago, Kebayoran Baru lost its allure to the more monied districts like Kemang and Simpruk.

Cozy restaurants, night spots, even New York delis are also sprinkled around these plush southern suburbs. In Pondok Indah, an American-style suburb wrapped around a first class golf course and country club, the size of the homes and estates would humble the homeowners of Bel Air in California.

For travelers who have neither the time nor the sense of adventure to explore some of the more remote corners of the nation, a park in south Jakarta provides a vicarious trip through the archipelago. Taman Mini Indonesia Indah ("Beautiful Indonesia in Miniature") is a cultural showcase nurtured by the President's wife, Madame Tien Suharto, that opened in 1975. All of the archipelago's architectural styles, as well as all the boundless creativity of its people, their crafts, music and dance, bubble through Taman Mini.

The best time to visit is on Sunday when thousands of Indonesians flock to the park. Whole families, representing many of the cultures represented at Taman Mini, lug baskets of food and thermos bottles of drinks and an armful of children. Whole families arrive on a single motorcycle, mother riding pillion with a child, another child or two straddling the gas tank. Seven or eight people or more crawl out of a compact Nissan taxi. The people love to gawk at foreigners, but feel free to gawk back.

Some of the groups head straight for the areas of the park that depict the provinces where they lived before moving to Jakarta. They watch a performance of a Manadonese Cakalele from North Sulawesi or a Balinese mask dance. They stare at the *prahu*-shaped houses in Torajaland, giggle at the gruesome woodcarvings that stare back at them in Irian Jaya, and sway along to the Ramayana ballet of East Java.

But most of all they stare curiously at each other and marvel at the miracle of the nation they have wrought from a tepid sea strewn with exotic islands. For Jakarta is the real *Taman Mini*, a microcosm of the very best that Indonesia has to offer.

*Among the newest attractions at Taman Mini Indonesia Indah is Keong Mas, named for its resemblance to a golden snail, which features a spectacular film of the wonders of Indonesia on the world's largest Imax screen.*

79

# Back of the Book

This back of the book section was designed to help you enhance your travel experience with detailed information, exciting insights and entertaining tidbits about Jakarta. There are maps of the city and its environs. Little known facts about Jakarta are brought to light in *Jakarta Trivia*. Suggested tours, with helpful maps, help you get around Old Batavia, Merdeka Square, Pasar Cikini, some of the antique stores, and Taman Mini Indonesia. *Off the Beaten Track* tells you how to get to some of the intriguing, lesser known points of interest in and around Jakarta. *Best Bets* is your guide to the very best the city has to offer — from penthouse suites to food stalls. Finally, *Travel Notes* lists the basic information needed to enjoy Jakarta.

*The grimacing monument in the center of the Kebayoran Baru traffic circle is officially called the Youth Statue, but is humorously nicknamed the "Pizza Man" or "Hot-Hands Harry."*

# JAKARTA

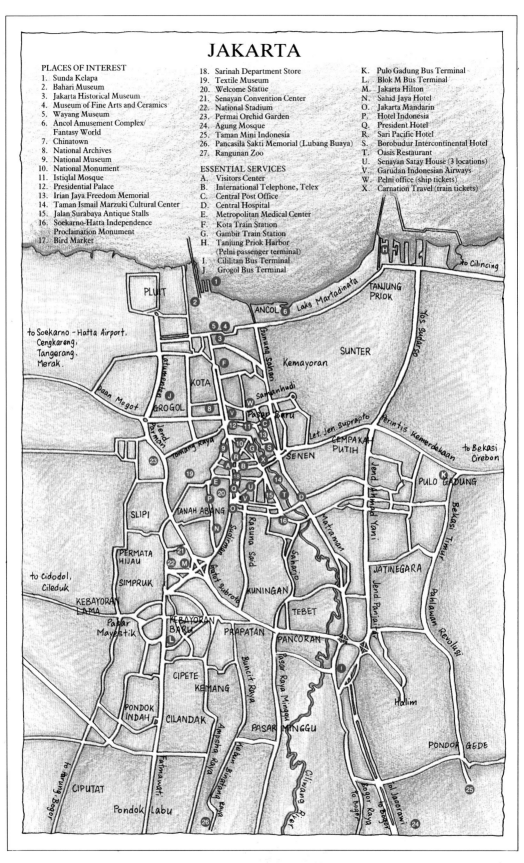

**PLACES OF INTEREST**
1. Sunda Kelapa
2. Bahari Museum
3. Jakarta Historical Museum
4. Museum of Fine Arts and Ceramics
5. Wayang Museum
6. Ancol Amusement Complex/
   Fantasy World
7. Chinatown
8. National Archives
9. National Museum
10. National Monument
11. Istiqlal Mosque
12. Presidential Palace
13. Irian Jaya Freedom Memorial
14. Taman Ismail Marzuki Cultural Center
15. Jalan Surabaya Antique Stalls
16. Soekarno-Hatta Independence
    Proclamation Monument
17. Bird Market

18. Sarinah Department Store
19. Textile Museum
20. Welcome Statue
21. Senayan Convention Center
22. National Stadium
23. Permai Orchid Garden
24. Agung Mosque
25. Taman Mini Indonesia
26. Pancasila Sakti Memorial (Lubang Buaya)
27. Rangunan Zoo

**ESSENTIAL SERVICES**
A. Visitors Center
B. International Telephone, Telex
C. Central Post Office
D. Central Hospital
E. Metropolitan Medical Center
F. Kota Train Station
G. Gambir Train Station
H. Tanjung Priok Harbor
   (Pelni passenger terminal)
I. Cililitan Bus Terminal
J. Grogol Bus Terminal

K. Pulo Gadung Bus Terminal
L. Blok M Bus Terminal
M. Jakarta Hilton
N. Sahid Jaya Hotel
O. Jakarta Mandarin
P. Hotel Indonesia
Q. President Hotel
R. Sari Pacific Hotel
S. Borobudur Intercontinental Hotel
T. Oasis Restaurant
U. Senayan Satay House (3 locations)
V. Garudan Indonesian Airways
W. Pelni office (ship tickets)
X. Carnation Travel (train tickets)

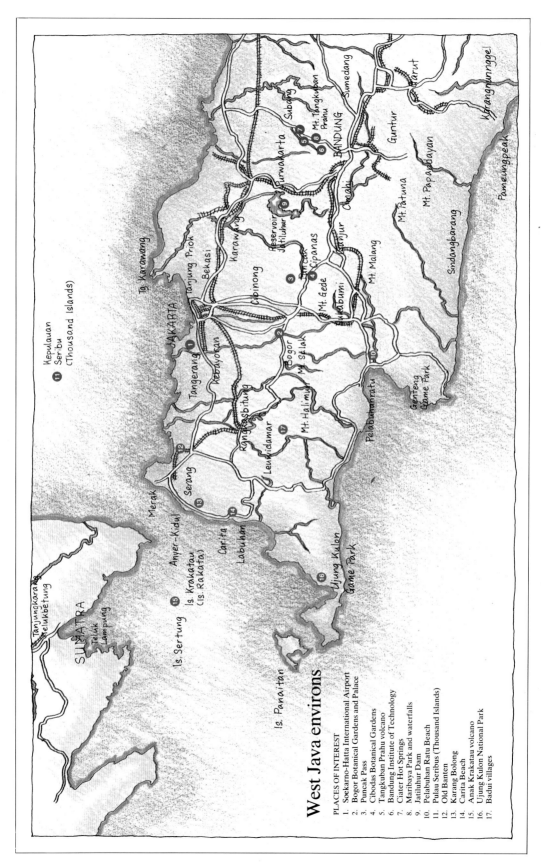

# West Java environs

PLACES OF INTEREST

1. Soekarno-Hatta International Airport
2. Bogor Botanical Gardens and Palace
3. Puncak Pass
4. Cibodas Botanical Gardens
5. Tangkuban Prahu volcano
6. Bandung Institute of Technology
7. Ciater Hot Springs
8. Jatiluhur Dam
9. Maribaya Park and waterfalls
10. Pelabuhan Ratu Beach
11. Pulau Seribu (Thousand Islands)
12. Old Banten
13. Karang Bolong
14. Carita Beach
15. Anak Krakatau volcano
16. Ujung Kulon National Park
17. Badui villages

83

# Jakarta Trivia

**LARGER THAN LIFE.** The 31st edition of the Guinness Book of World Records lists the Keong Mas (Golden Snail) Imax Theater in Jakarta's Taman Mini Indonesia Indah as the world's largest permanently-installed movie screen. According to the record book, the screen (made in England) measures 29.26 meters tall by 24.48 meters wide. That makes it almost the same height as a 10-storey building. Don't miss the "Beautiful Indonesia" film which features some of the most spectacular footage of the islands ever filmed. The enormous screen adds a dramatic dimension to the sweeping panoramas of fuming volcanos, swirling padi fields and heavenly seas. Screened daily at 12, 2 and 4 p.m. and every hour on Sundays from 10 a.m. to 5 p.m. On Saturdays there is another feature entitled "To Fly". The theater takes its name from its snailshell shape and its gold-colored ceramic tiles. The snail plays an important role in Javanese fairy tales.

**GOING MOBILE.** Jakarta's car population is increasing by 14 per cent annually, one of the fastest growth rates of vehicles in the developing world (which helps explain the city's horrendous traffic jams). As of 1986, there were more than one million motor vehicles in the city consuming more than ten million liters of fuel every day.

**WHAT'S IN A NAME.** The address where a food stall originated is often found in its name. For example, *Gado-Gado Cemara* (aficionados consider it Jakarta's best *gado-gado* — greens and rice cakes topped with peanut sauce — in town) now found in front of Pasar Boplo on Jalan Srikaya was located on Jalan Cemara until it moved to make way for the widening of the road. In this manner, many *warung* are able to keep their old clientele from losing track of their whereabouts. *Gado-Gado Cemara's* secret, by the way, is in its peanut sauce. The roadside cafe's chef makes it from ground cashews.

**BIG STATISTICS.** Jakarta is the capital of the world's largest archipelago. Boasting a usually quoted figure of 13,677 islands, Indonesia measures 5,120 kilometers from its westernmost point at Sabang on Weh Island west of the Malaysian peninsula to its eastern corner at Merauke in the province of Irian Jaya on the island of New Guinea. Three of those islands — New Guinea, Borneo and Sumatra — rank among the top five in the world in size. The total population of the archipelago is estimated at 165 million, which makes Indonesia the fifth most populous country in the world, exceeded only by China, India, the Soviet Union and the United States. The island of Java, where Jakarta is located, is home to the largest proportion of people. Some 100 million are packed into the island which is about the same size as Greece, a nation of 10 million, making Java one of the world's most densely-populated pieces of real estate. At least 90 per cent of the population nominally subscribes to Islam. That means Indonesia has more Muslims than any other nation in the world.

**MASSIVE MOVEMENT.** In an effort to ease overcrowding in Jakarta and other parts of Java, the Indonesian government has embarked on an ambitious program, called transmigration, aimed at trying to spread people out among some of the less populated islands. (People live on only about 3,000 of the archipelago's islands and, in contrast to Java, the Indonesian portions of the huge islands of Borneo and New Guinea rank among the world's least densely-populated pieces of real estate). With the aid of funding from the World Bank and European Economic Community development fund, about three million people have been moved to outer islands since the program began in earnest in 1969 and the government expects to increase the pace of movement to nearly 800,000 people annually by the end of the decade. Volunteers for the program are attracted by free transportation, housing, the deed to 2.5 hectares of land, shared livestock and three years worth of basic provisions and tools and the prospect of starting new lives as pioneers of the nation's vast frontiers. Indonesian officials are realistic enough to realize that even transmigration will not make much of a dent in Java's ever-burgeoning population. But they view the program as a means of opening up the nation's wildernesses to development.

**ISLAND FOR LOST SOULS.** Like many bustling metropolises, Jakarta has its share of underemployed and unskilled squatters who turn to begging to survive. In an effort to curb the problem, the government has set aside an area on Tidung Kecil, one of the Thousand Islands in Jakarta Bay, as a training ground for upgrading the skills of "beggars and loafers". The center will cater to up to 100 people simultaneously, teaching them some of the skills of agriculture and fish breeding, among others that will prove useful and productive.

**FROM NIGHTMARE TO PLEASANT DREAMS.** Up until the middle of the 1960s, the site of the Taman Impian Jaya Ancol recreation complex was 552 acres of malarial mosquito-infested swamp. The government-ordered reclamation of the marshland began in 1962 and was completed in 1966. Taman Impian Jaya Ancol, which translates simply and appropriately into "Dreamland", opened in 1967 with one modest night club, a go-kart track and beach recreational facilities. Since then it has rapidly expanded into one of the most comprehensive recreation centers in Asia and attracts some 15 million visitors annually, about the same number that visit Walt Disney World in the U.S. every year.

The facilities include a golf course, marina, the Pasar Seni arts and crafts market, night clubs, extensive swimming facilities and water sports equipment, the 350 room Horizon Hotel, numerous restaurants and food stalls, and Southeast Asia's largest drive-in theater which screens three films nightly, four on weekends, to a capacity of 850 automobiles. In 1985, Asia's most sophisticated amusement park outside Japan, *Dunia Fantasie*, "Fantasy World", opened its gates at Dreamland.

**PIRATED AID.** Don't look for copied recordings of the "Live Aid" concert in Jakarta's thriving music cassette stores. The city's notorious "music pirates" made expert recordings of the 1985 "Live Aid" concert, televised to millions worldwide to raise money for victims of famine in Africa. Multiple cassette sets of the concert were popular sellers but were pulled off the market after "Live Aid" organizer Bob Geldof complained to the Indonesian government that the "music pirates" were literally taking food from the mouths of famine victims. Geldof said about 1.5 million Indonesian-made tapes of the concert had been sold in Southeast Asia and the Middle East earning "pirates" some U.S. $3 million. However, one local musical group later proved that the vast majority of Indonesians have their hearts in the right place. The group, Bimbo, recorded an Indonesian song called *Kita Adalah Satu* ("We Are One") that was inspired by "We Are the World". The sale of 100,000 copies of the cassette earned Rp25 million for Jakarta's Center for Handicapped Children.

**21ST CENTURY SUPER CITY.** Farsighted city planners have already drawn up plans that will transform Jakarta into a massive megalopolis called Jabotabek by the turn of the century. Jabotabek is an acronym made up of the name of Jakarta and of the surrounding cities — Bogor to the south, Tangerang in the west, and Bekasi in the East — that will become part of the enormous 21st century city. The authorities envision Jabotabek covering more than 7,500 square miles and having a staggering population of 25 million by the year 2005. Plans call for the construction of new residential areas with adjoining industrial office parks in outlying areas linked to the downtown area by a series of ring roads and expressways. It is hoped the plan will reduce the concentration of people in the city center from 90 per cent of the total population at present to a more manageable 63 per cent.

**THE HAWAIIAN CONNECTION.** The venerable ukulele, usually associated with the lilting music of the Hawaiian islands, is closely-related and possibly even a direct descendant of the *keroncong* instruments of Jakarta. The original *keroncong*, a small guitar brought to the island by the Portuguese in the

16th century to play their Moorish-style music, had a beautifully-shaped bulging back. But it later evolved into a simpler instrument with a flat back that is identical to the ukulele of Hawaii. Other instruments used in the *keroncong* orchestras of Jakarta, that once played at the Capitol Restaurant in Jalan Pintu Air and the night markets in Gambir Square, include a *rebana* (a kind of tambourine), a violin, a type of mandolin called the *macinas*, flutes and violincello. Musicians have exported their popular *keroncong* music throughout the archipelago. Aside from musical instruments, anthropologists suspect that ancient peoples from Southeast Asia carried many of their traditions and customs with them as they spread through the Indonesian islands, then on through Polynesia and Hawaii. There are remarkable similarities between dress, weapons and some customs in parts of Indonesia, particularly the Moluccas, and Hawaii.

**FORGOTTEN FOUNDER.** Dutch East India Company mogul, Jan Pieterszoon Coen (1587–1629), founded modern Jakarta when he seized it in 1619 and laid the groundwork that made the city the capital of modern Indonesia. But today there are no monuments in the city to commemorate his achievements. A bronze statue of Coen once stood in front of the Harmonie Club, in its heyday the colonial center of Batavia, but like the club itself, has disappeared. Another statue of Coen once stood in front of the Supreme Court building across the street from the Hotel Borobudur Intercontinental, but the Japanese melted it down for scrap metal during their World War II occupation of the city. Historians generally agree that Coen was a ruthless tyrant, infamous for his brutal treatment of local people, so it is understandable why the Indonesians do not honor his memory. Even Coen's grave has been lost to the ravages of time and, perhaps, hard feelings. After his death, apparently of cholera, he was buried by his fellow Dutchmen in a magnificent funeral ceremony in the City Hall. His remains were later transferred to the site of the Dutch Reformed Church that once stood where the Wayang Museum now stands. But there was no marker or relic preserved when that church was razed 200 years later, although it is generally agreed that the grounds of the museum were Coen's last resting place.

**WHAT'S IN A NAME, PART II.** President Sukarno named Sarinah Department Store, built in the early 1960s, after his nursemaid.

**LAND OF THE LIVING.** Dying in Jakarta can prove just as challenging as living in the city. The government has problems finding room to bury the 150 to 200 people who pass away in Jakarta every day. In fact, a local ordinance limits the time the

deceased is entitled to remain in his grave to three years, although extensions are permitted. City officials have appealed to residents not to overuse the extension to allow others a chance of burial.

**TEED OFF WITH CHARM.** Swingers at the Rawamangun Golf Course can keep their eye on the ball, instead of the bushes, thanks to the effort of a snake charmer. When the President of the Jakarta Golf Club, Minister of Manpower Sudomo, ordered the course cleared of the scaly creatures, many of them poisonous, a snake charmer from Central Java was summoned to do the job. Sutono, bagged hundreds of snakes and took them to Semarang where he is in charge of the area snake section. "Anyone can charm snakes away if they practice communicating with animals," said Sutono.

**TASTY CURES.** Visitors to Jakarta who suffer from rheumatism, gout and eczema should try the "medicinal" food stalls at the Lokasari area in the vicinity of Jalan Raya Mangga Besar in Kota. Some of the exotic concoctions served at the park are said to have curative powers that may be able to help — if they don't make you sick to your stomach first. The banner strung over the entrance of one stall translates as: "All kinds of soups — crocodile, iguana, bat, snake, monkey and anteater."

**HALFWAY HOUSE.** Jakarta's ubiquitous *waria*, also known as *bancis*, are the target of active socialization programs aimed at helping them cope with the problems caused by their sexual handicap. According to Nurlaila Sari, head of West Jakarta's *waria* organization, her group aims to help the physically hermaphrodite who have mentally assumed the "women's role". A *Waria* Rehabilitation Night has been held at the Senayan Convention Hall, *waria* beauty contests have been held regularly and a *waria* center is planned.

**HEAVEN SCENT.** Notice a pleasant aroma in the air of Jakarta? It probably emanates from a local type of cigarette called *kretek*, which gets its intoxicating fragrance from cloves. Despite the known health problems caused by cigarettes, the *kretek* is an Indonesian passion. Each day, millions of *kretek* cigarettes are rolled by hand and machine in enormous factories, mainly in Kudus in Central Java and Kediri in East Java, and sold in Indonesia and exported under brand names like *Gudang Garam* and *Djarum*. *Kretek* have an almost fanatic following among smokers in many other countries. Cloves, blended with tobacco grown in the highlands of Central Java, are endemic to the Moluccas islands which became known as the *Spice Islands*. Prized by the Han court in China as a breath freshener, most European countries fought for control of the spice trade in the Moluccas in the 16th century when cloves were literally worth their weight in gold. After the Dutch gained control, cloves rapidly declined in importance. The Dutch eventually introduced cigarettes composed of a local tobacco spiced with cloves in a 2:1 mixture to encourage Indonesians to smoke cigarettes as an alternative to chewing betel nuts. Ternate, Ambon and other islands in the Moluccas still have thriving clove plantations, but are unable to fulfill the demand by the *kretek* industry.

**TEA AND LOTTERY.** Some Jakarta housewives liven up their morning coffee get-togethers with a lottery called *arisan*. Each visitor puts money in a pot during each session, a drawing is held and one lucky lady goes home with all the loot afterwards. Genteel ladies steadfastly deny that *Arisan* is a friendly form of gambling, much like *mahjong*, but prefer to characterize it as "banking between friends". However, *arisan* is taken quite seriously in some sectors. A leading local television actress committed suicide after she reportedly told friends that she owed her *arisan* friends Rp5 million.

**MELTING POT.** The majority of Jakarta's adult population were not born in the city. Most came to the capital from other parts of Indonesia only after independence in 1945.

## Jakarta Tours

**BACK IN OLD BATAVIA.** An easy, sensory-stimulating walk around the north central part of the city will propel you back in time, as far back as 500 years ago when colonial maritime powers transformed Jakarta into a strategic base for the lucrative spice trade. The walk starts in Sunda Kelapa, the old port used by the Hindu kings prior to the 16th century and later by the Portuguese and Dutch. Old Batavia grew up around Sunda Kelapa after the conquest of Jan Pieterszoon Coen and the Dutch East Indies Company.

At the corner of Jalan Pakin, climb to the top of the Harbor Master Tower (**1**), *Uitkijk* in Dutch and *Menara Sahbandar* in Indonesian, for a panoramic view of Jakarta's oldest quarter. Repaired and refitted in 1977 as part of the Old Batavia restoration program, the tower itself dates back only to 1839. The coralstone base from which it rises was laid in 1645 and was a corner bastion of the walls that enclosed the oldest Dutch section of the city.

If you can stomach the smell and the flies, visit *Pasar Ikan*, the Fish market (**2**), a few steps northwest of the tower which operates much as it has for centuries. The best time to visit is early morning when fishermen bring in their evening catch and women haggle over the price of the fresh seafood. The market's retail section sells everything needed to equip a fishing boat, handmade household items, wooden trucks and more traditional toys and *keroncong* musical instruments.

Follow the stone wall (**3**) on your right on the walk from the fish market. It was the fortified wall of Dutch warehouses, first erected in 1652 but reconstructed several times through the centuries. Armed soldiers once patroled the walls, guarding the mace, nutmeg, pepper, cloves, coffee, tea, cloth and other booty inside the warehouses before it was loaded on ships bound for the Middle East and Europe. Now the *Bahari Museum* (**4**) is located within its walls, displaying old maps of Old Batavia and miniature models of Indonesian sailing vessels. The crumbling remains of the fortification that once surrounded all of Old Batavia can be traced by continuing to follow the wall west. Only two of the original 15 bastions are still intact.

Back behind the Harbor Master Tower, cross the small bridge and walk toward the pier. Buy a ticket from the port office to pass through a police checkpoint and walk out to the piers to see what is left of Sunda Kelapa (**5**). Crowded with elegant Bugis *pinisi* schooners, it remains one of the most impressive sights in the city.

Across Jalan Pakin, paralleling Jalan Nelayan Timur 300 meters south of the tower, is a nicely-restored drawbridge (**6**), the last of a series that once lined *Kali Besar*, the "Big Canal." Believed to

be more than 200 years old, the Dutch called it *Hoenderpasarbrug*, the "Chickenmarket Bridge."

About 500 meters south of the bridge, on the west side of the canal, are two of the area's oldest structures that typify residential architecture used within Old Batavia's walls. The building at Jalan Kali Besar Barat No. 11, now called *Toko Merah* (**7**), Red Store, was built around 1730. Comprising two residences, the northern half was once the home of Gustaff Willem van Imhoff, Governor-General of Batavia from 1743 to 1750. Three doors south, the handsome yellow building now used by Chartered Bank (**8**) also dates back to the early 18th century. It was restored in 1921.

Almost due east from these old homes, down Jalan Kali Besar Timur V, is Taman Fatahillah, the centerpiece of the Old Batavia restoration. The most imposing building on the cobblestone plaza, anchored by a copy of a 17th century fountain, is the *Stadhuis* (**9**) or City Hall. This is the third

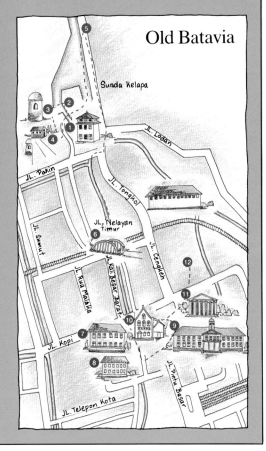

Old Batavia

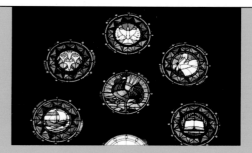

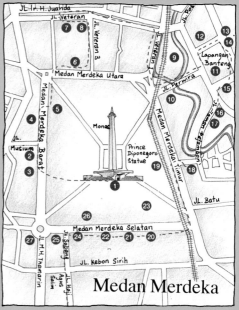

Medan Merdeka

version of the administrative headquarters that have occupied the spot since 1620, the year after Coen seized the city. Completed in 1710, the design was a provincial version of the city hall in Amsterdam. It has been in continuous use for more than two-and-a-half centuries and now houses the Jakarta Historical Museum.

Just west of City Hall at Jalan Pintu Besar Utara 27 is the Wayang Museum (10). Although the building and its facade were built early this century, it sits on the foundation of important old Dutch Reformed churches first constructed in 1640. In fact, in the midst of the displays of Indonesia's puppet crafts are some of the tombstones of important Dutch officials that were buried in the churches. Coen is said to have been buried here.

The Neoclassical building on the east side of Taman Fatahillah is the *Balai Seni Rupa*, Museum of Fine Arts (11). Completed in 1870, it was formerly the Hall of Justice.

Wind up your tour of Old Batavia with a look at *Si Jagur* (12) also known as *Kyai Jagur,* the big bronze cannon on the north side of the square with the obscene fist on its loading muzzle. Ladies who are not in the market for a child should avoid sitting on it to have their picture taken, however.

**AROUND MEDAN MERDEKA.** This long hike around the administrative heart of the Indonesian nation begins at Jakarta's most conspicuous landmark, the National Monument (1), a white marble obelisk called *Monas*, for short. Built by Sukarno as a testament to the strength of the Republic (and, some say, his own virility), Monas rises 137 meters into the sultry skies. For a small entrance fee, you can ride an elevator to the top for a good look out at the city and sea and up at the 35 kilograms of gold leaf on the monument's flame. The 48 dioramas on the base of the monument relate the history of Indonesia from Java Man to the New Order government. There is also a Hall of Silence that features a gilded map of Indonesia and the national insignia of the Garuda. A golden tabernacle opens to reveal the original Declaration of Independence, while a recording plays back Sukarno's voice reading the proclamation.

*Monas* is located at the center of Medan Merdeka, the neatly-landscaped "Independence Field" that is almost a square kilometer in area. The statue of a man on a horse in front of *Monas* is national hero Prince Diponegoro. From *Monas*, walk west and cross the wide, busy lanes of Jalan Medan Merdeka Barat (please use the crosswalk). The building with the rounded portico, Doric columns and statue of an elephant (a gift from King Chulalongkorn of Siam in 1871) on the corner of Jalan Musium is the National Museum (2). You may wish to spend a few

hours examining its excellent archaeological and ethnographic collections.

Left of the museum is the Department of Defense (3) built in 1928 as a law school. Walk north across Jalan Musium, past Radio Republik Indonesia (4), formerly the Netherlands Indies Broadcasting Building. Looking back across toward Monas, you will see *Air Mancur Menari* (5), the Dancing Fountain. Illuminated with colored lights, the water spurts to the rhythm of music during performances that are held each evening.

Continue to the northern boundary of the square, Jalan Medan Merdeka Utara. The building with the Corinthian pillars that bears a resemblance to Washington's White House is the *Istana Merdeka* (6), Independence Palace. Built in 1861, it was used as the presidential residence by Sukarno. President Suharto, however, lives in Menteng and uses the palace for ceremonial functions. Important state visitors stay in a guest house behind it. For a good look at the older *State Palace* (7), built at the end of the 18th century as a country house and connected to *Istana Merdeka* by a garden, walk down Jalan Veteran 3 and turn left on the usually jammed Jalan Veteran and pass Bina Graha (8), the presidential office building. This road, now cluttered with office buildings and restaurants, was the heart of the posh Weltevreden (Dutch for "well-content") district during the colonial heyday.

Then retrace your steps east and cross Jalan

Veteran 3 to Jalan Veteran 1. Turn right back toward Medan Merdeka passing the imposing white dome and futuristic minaret of the enormous, national Istiqlal Mosque (9) opened in 1978 after a decade of construction. If you wish to have a look inside, make sure you leave your shoes at the door before entering. Women and men must be properly attired and observe Islamic etiquette.

Staying on Jalan Medan Merdeka Timur, cross the railroad tracks (carefully) and turn left on Jalan Perwira with the mosque still on your left. The gleaming white central office tower of Pertamina (10), the national oil company, rises importantly across the street. Indonesia is the region's largest oil producer and an influential member of OPEC.

Dead ahead is Lapangan Banteng (11), laid out during the time of Napoleon-appointed Governor-General, Herman Daendels as Waterloo Square. The muscular statue with the tortured face in the square commemorates Indonesia's liberation of Irian Jaya, formerly Dutch New Guinea.

Around the square is a Neo-Gothic Roman Catholic Cathedral (12) of early 20th century vintage on the northern corner. Turn right and right again, past the *kakilima* (street vendors), and walk past the Ministry of Finance (13). Daendels began building it in Empire style in 1809 as a palace but it never served that purpose. To its north is another Neoclassical edifice built in 1848 that is now Mahkamah Agung (14), the Supreme Court.

At this point, you will be overdue for an air-conditioned break and the solid, if oppressive-looking, Borobudur Intercontinental Hotel (15) in front of you is the place for that. The coffee shop has a section that specializes in spicy Indonesian soups and light, restoration dishes.

Afterwards, walk right from the hotel entrance to Jalan Pejambon. Adjacent to the modern office blocks of the Ministry of Foreign Affairs, (16) *Department Luar Negeri*, is a small building with a facade of Ionic columns and pilasters. This is *Gedung Pancasila* (17). In 1914, it housed the *Volksraad*, the "People's Council" that became a platform for Indonesian nationalists. Here, on July 1, 1945, Sukarno introduced his five principles of Pancasila, Indonesia's national philosophy.

At the corner of Jalan Pejambon and Jalan Medan Merdeka Timur is a circular-shaped church, Gereja Emmanuel (18). It was built in 1835 for Dutch Protestants and some of the antique furnishings inside are as old as the church. The Gambir Railway Station (19) is across the multi-laned street. Turn left (south) then right (west) on to Jalan Medan Merdeka Selatan. You will pass the fortified, undistinguished compound of the American Embassy (20), the distinguished Vice Presidential

office (21), the contemporary tower and office complex of Jakarta's City Hall, DKI, (22), the Jakarta Fairgrounds (23), the Stock Exchange or *Gedung Bursa* (24), and tall Wisma Antara, (25) home of Bank of America, the national Indonesian news agency and the offices of many foreign news agencies. There is a small children's amusement park, Taman Ria (26), across the roundabout to the north, and the solid-looking Bank Indonesia (27) on the west side. From Wisma Antara, walk south on Jalan Sabang and Agus Salim. The latter has many bakeries and restaurants featuring everything from *padang* to fast food and lots of photo stores.

**PASAR CIKINI.** Despite the onslaught of 20th century fast food and smog, the exotic oriental tastes and aromas that seem to emanate straight from the pages of a Joseph Conrad novel have managed to endure in Jakarta. To immerse yourself in them, try Pasar Cikini (*pasar* is Indonesian for market), a sensational culinary treat on Jalan Pegangasan Timur, conveniently located across the railroad tracks on the eastern boundary of the pleasant Menteng district. As with most of Indonesia's traditional markets, the best time to visit is during the hustle-and-bustle of early morning.

The entrance to the *pasar* (1) is an awesome display of contemporary-capitalism-gone-berserk. Sidewalks are buried under tons of cheap, colorful children's toys (almost all under Rp2,000), plastic housewares and genuine imitations of designer sunglasses, watches and the like.

If you manage to excavate your way through the merchandise and crowds to the interior, stop and take in the panoramic view (2) of the tropical fruits that seemingly reach to the horizon. Even some recognizable varieties may look unrecognizable in this part of the world. For instance, you will find dozens of kinds of bananas alone. (Indonesia boasts more than 100 species!)

Fresh roots and tubers are sold at the same stalls as the dried spices (3). The black pepper, coriander, cumin, cinnamon, cloves, nutmeg, mace and others spices that inspired fantastic stories and markets in Europe centuries ago, and changed the course of history, can all be found in this section.

Beyond the fruit stalls is the fresh produce section (4), heaped with mountains of tropical and temperate vegetables. The latter are raised in the cool highlands south of Jakarta. Most kinds of vegetables are plentiful year-round, although prolonged dry spells or heavy rains can produce shortages.

The rear of Pasar Cikini is reserved for the lively trade in fish and seafood (5). Follow the smell to popular local varieties including *kakap* (a saltwater perch), *ikan merah* (red snapper) and *ikan mas* (translates as goldfish, but is actually a freshwater

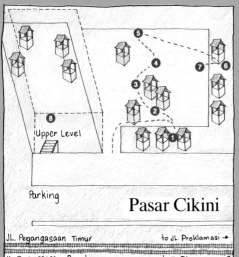

Pasar Cikini

JL. Pegangasaan Timur    to JL. Proklamasi →

JL. Pegangasaan Barat    to JL. Diponegoro ⤴

carp). *Udang* (prawns), *kepiting* (crab), and *cumi-cumi* (squid) are also popular in most of Indonesia.

From the fish market proceed to the south side of Pasar Cikini (**6**) where you will find a long row of small Chinese-operated shops doing a busy retail business. Out front a vast collection of crackers and chips that pop into airy, edible sculptures when dropped in hot oil and go by the collective name of *krupuk* are sold in open bins.

Buy a "cuppa of Java" — select a half kilo each of *robusta*, the slightly bitter coffee beans, and *arabica*, the smooth rich variety, and blend before grinding. Also in this section you will find electric coconut grinders grating the meat from mature coconut pods. The grated coconut is "milked" for its rich liquids, commonly used in curries and sweet foods.

The utensils used to create an Indonesian feast are sold behind the Chinese shops (**7**): handmade baskets and mats, used for different steps of food processing and for serving; a stone mortar and pestle for grinding fresh spices; and terracotta earthen pots used as "slow-cookers" for mellowing a good curry. The ever popular Indonesian barbequed satay requires a full set of special equipment.

Finally, the second floor of Pasar Cikini houses the Gold Market (**8**). Dozens of small shops sell gold jewelry and bars for only a fraction more than the daily price of the metal.

**AROUND THE SHOPS.** Jakarta's best browse-and-buy spots are sprinkled throughout the city, thus it will be necessary to travel between them by taxi. Better yet, hire a *taxi gelap* or "dark taxi" (about Rp4,000 per hour, minimum two hours including air conditioning). These freelance cars and drivers can be found waiting for passengers at the carpark south of the Kartika Plaza Hotel on Jalan Jenderal Sudirman or on Jalan Kediri behind the Menteng football field. Those who like to linger as they look and wish to avoid exotical overload should spread out visits over two or three mornings, taking in one or two of the shopping areas at a time.

First stop is the city's most famous, and simultaneously infamous, shopping street, the *Barang-Barang Antik* (**1**) on Jalan Surabaya. This megamart stretches north to south from Jalan Professor Mohammed Yamin to Jalan Diponegoro where it deteriorates into a jungle of stalls selling cheap luggage. Do not go expecting to find an ancient rare *kris* dagger or other potentially lucrative artifact at a low price. You are not likely to. What you will find are 30 stalls offering a lot of "antiques" that were probably made in the salesmen's *kampungs* last week. Genuine antiques, however, can be found.

A safer bet for those searching for genuine antiques, but with genuine antique prices, is a row of shops not far northeast of Medan Merdeka: N.V. Garuda Antiques (**2**), Jalan Majapahit 12; Arjuna Art & Curio (**3**), Jalan Majapahit 16A N.V. (good selection of bronze and porcelain); Lee Cheong (**4**), Jalan Majapahit 32; and Polim's (**5**), across the street at Jalan Gajah Mada 126.

Likewise, a narrow street off Jalan Kebon Sirih, just west of the Hyatt Hotel, has several reliable antique stores frequented by professional dealers. At Djoby's (**6**), Jalan Kebon Sirih Timur Dalam 22, Pak Nasir will explain the mysteries of primitive Indonesian art. Ask to see his exquisite selection of ancient textiles. Look at silver items that include belts used by traditional classical dancers in Java and Bali. Like most shops on this street, Djody's accepts credit cards. Nasrun Antique, Art and Curio (**7**), Jalan Kebon Sirih Timur 39, has a beautiful collection of kris, the traditional daggers of the Malays that many people still believe to be magical. The kris, which usually has an artistically-decorated sheath, must be properly protected and handled. Make sure you listen to instructions carefully after purchasing one to avoid adverse spiritual manifestations when you get it home!

Another row of antique shops has sprung up in Blok M in Kebayoran Baru. There is a wide range of old furniture and excellent quality copies of furniture from Indonesia and other Asian countries at Royal Store (**8**), Jalan Palatehan I/36. Next door at Jalan Palatehan I/37 is the Djelita Art Shop (**9**), which offers a wide range of handicrafts including puppets, statues and batik paintings. Hadiparana Galleries (**10**), Jalan Palatehan I/38, has a good selection of modern silver jewelry, wood carvings, contemporary paintings and silk batik. Expensive,

but very good quality. Urip Store (11), Jalan Palatehan I/41, specializes in primitive art, antique furniture, textiles and silverwork. Pigura Arts and Crafts (12), Jalan Palatehan I/41, has carvings, bronzeware, ceramics and leather goods. Pura Art Shop (13), Jalan Palatehan I/43, features tin products from the Bangka Islands and some great Balinese and Javanese dance masks. A bit south, behind the Sarinah Jaya Department Store, is Majapahit Art and Curio (14), Jalan Melawai III/4.

By far Jakarta's best arts and crafts mart in a clean pleasant setting is Pasar Seni (15) in the Jaya Ancol Dreamland recreation complex. Cooled by the balmy breezes off Jakarta Bay, you can watch painters, wood carvers, batik makers, silversmiths, puppet makers and other craftsmen from many parts of Indonesia at work. Look for the tin-toy stall where an ingenious artisan creates miniature masterpieces from discarded tin cans and other recycled junk. Pasar Seni also has a variety of restaurants and stalls featuring authentic Indonesian cuisine and eminently edible snacks.

Another pleasant complex for shopping, snacking and just absorbing the aromas of the tropics, is the Indonesian Bazaar on the sprawling grounds (16) of the Jakarta Hilton Hotel. A variety of shops here sell fine jewelry, batik clothing, paintings and other local products along a lovely lagoon where swans and geese play. Most are open from 10 a.m. to 6 p.m. Smack in the middle of the Bazaar is the Pizza Ria which has authentic, inexpensive Italian food and nightly entertainment.

Finally, the granddaddy of Jakarta's department stores, Sarinah, on Jalan Thamrin (17) and at Blok M (18), has entire floors crammed with affordable, quality handicrafts from the entire archipelago.

**THROUGH TAMAN MINI INDONESIA INDAH.**
Few visitors to Jakarta, indeed, few Indonesians, ever travel the length and breadth of the nation's vast archipelago. A vicarious tour through all of the nation's 27 provinces and special administrative districts and a sampling of their more than 300 cultures is possible, however, without even venturing beyond the capital.

Taman Mini Indonesia Indah, "Beautiful Indonesia in Miniature," showcases the architecture, cultures, cuisine and arts of the islands in some 300 hectares of pavilions, exhibits, museums, dioramas, rides and other attractions. Opened in 1975, Taman Mini was nurtured by Indonesia's First Lady Ibu Siti Hartinah Suharto who is taking an interest in the continuing expansion of its features and facilities. Most live performances occur on Sundays, but that is also the most crowded day so you may wish to spread your visit across two days — one a quiet weekday when you concentrate on the exhibits and

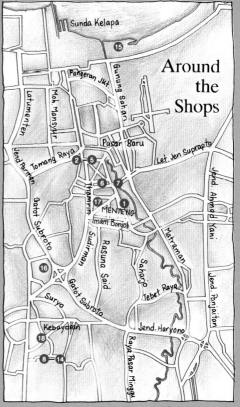

Around the Shops

a Sunday to catch some of the music and dance.

Take a taxi to the park's gates located off the first exit of the Jagowari Toll Road. From there you can get around inside the huge park either on foot, train, horse carriage or cable car. A nominal entrance fee gets you inside and through most exhibits, but there are additional small fees for the transport and some of the other attractions inside.

The landmark in front is a scaled-down rendering of the National Monument (1) in Medan Merdeka. There is a contemporary version of a *pendopo* (2), a Javanese assembly hall, just beyond.

The recommended way to begin your tour is by viewing the spectacular Imax movie in Keong Mas (3), the building that looks like a golden snail, only Rp1,000. Next walk back past the entrance to Museum Indonesia (4), the country's best-displayed collection of artifacts and handicrafts. The building itself is a spectacular edifice in classical Balinese style with surrounding ponds and gardens.

Each floor of the museum has a separate theme that illustrates the life of the archipelago. The first

focuses on the national concept of *Bhinneka Tung-gal Ika*, "Unity Through Diversity," with a life-size Central Javanese wedding ceremony display. The wedding "guests," all in traditional costumes, represent each province.

Have a look at the paradisiacal, man-made swimming complex behind the museum (5) because you may want to come back to it after your walking tour "through the archipelago." Start the journey where you might if you were really hiking through the islands from Jakarta, at the subdivision representing Jambi (6) province in southernmost Sumatra. Then work your way systematically through that huge island's other provinces: Bengkulu (7), South Sumatra (8), the Riau island group (9), West Sumatra (10) with its immense Minangkabau dwelling, North Sumatra (11) and the fervently Islamic special district of Aceh (12). As you cover these regional subdivisions you will follow the bank of a lagoon (13) on your right. The clumps of land in the water are a man-made replica of the archipelago that can be viewed from the Skylift ride (enter at 14). Carrying a map of the archipelago will also enhance your understanding of Indonesia's geography as you tour the park.

Continuing your walking tour, however, the next group of "provinces" are those on the Indonesian portion of the island of Borneo: West Kalimantan (15), South Kalimantan (16), East Kalimantan with its traditional Dayak longhouse (17) and Central Kalimantan (18). In front of the latter is a compound representing Maluku (19) or the Moluccas, history's "Spice Islands."

Next you will come to two of the provinces of the island of Sulawesi: Utara or north (20) and Tengah or central (21). Wind up your stroll around the north side of Taman Mini inside the geodesic dome of the Aviary (22). At this point the children may

be ready for a ride on a merry-go-round or the other amusements of the Children's Palace (23) while parents can cool off at the artificial waterfall (24).

Resume your tour of the Indonesian archipelago in its newest most remote and primitive province, Irian Jaya (25), the western half of New Guinea island. Adjoining that is its newest province, East Timor (26). The other two provinces of Sulawesi, Tenggara (27) or southeast and Selatan (28), south, are the first provincial displays on the south side of the rectangular park.

The nearby building shaped like a dragon is the Komodo Museum (29). It highlights the archipelago's widely-varying tropical fauna. A smaller pavilion behind houses the Stamp Museum (30).

Double back down the lane to the displays of Indonesia's rarely-visited Lesser Sundas chain of islands: Nusa Tenggara Timur (31) and Nusa Tenggara Barat (32). Continuing west, you will see the unmistakable walled compound representing Bali (33). There are frequent performances of Bali's renowned dance and drama here.

The island you are standing on is represented by pavilions featuring East Java (34), the special district of Yogyakarta (35) which is the island's cultural heart, Central Java (36), West Java (37) and you wind up the long journey where you began in Jakarta (38). A bit out-of-place is Lampung (39) another province of Sumatra.

The structures on the southwest edge of the park exemplify Indonesia's national philosophy of Pancasila which recognizes five religions that worship one god: Islam, the Prince Diponegoro Mosque (40); Catholicism, the church (41); Protestantism, another church (42); Hinduism, a temple (43); and Buddhism, a *wihara* (44). Finally, there is a model of Central Java's remarkable 7th Century Borobudur (45), the world's largest Buddhist temple.

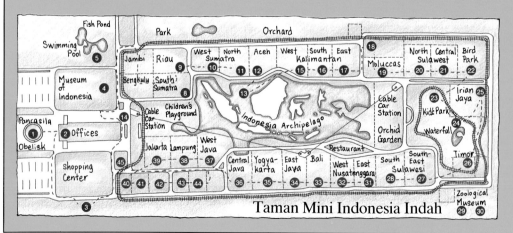

Taman Mini Indonesia Indah

## Off the Beaten Track

**MARVEL AT A GLORIOUS SUNRISE** amid Edelweiss flowers on the side of a volcano called Gunung Gede. Walk six hours through a rain forest in the moonlight on a trail that begins in the Cibodas Botanical Gardens, approximately 40 minutes from Jakarta via the Jagowari Toll Road. Best to rent car with driver. (Turn right on the marked road past Puncak Pass.) One side of the volcano fell away after an earthquake and formed a plateau called *Surya Kencana*, "Golden Sun". Another shorter trail from the park (about an hour-and-a-half each way) ends at a mossy rock wall splashed by the Ciboreum waterfalls. Best to rent a car with an experienced local driver.

**EVERGREEN HOTEL,** Jalan Puncak Raya 84, (Tel. Bogor 4075) is in the same vicinity, near tea plantations just before reaching Puncak Pass and just beyond Bogor. It has Olympic-sized, spring-fed pools where you can swim in the serene mountain setting that rises over the fields of tea.

**CONDET,** in southeast Jakarta, is a cultural preservation area where some of the Betawi (Indonesians with long time roots in Batavia) traditions and architectural styles are maintained. You can buy some of the tastiest *emping* crackers, made from hand-smashed *melinjo* nuts, from the residents here. Easy to get to by taxi.

**VISIT A BUGIS SAILING SCHOONER** at the history-rich port area of Sunda Kelapa. The Bugis, who have been sailing around the archipelago and beyond for centuries aboard these magnificent handbuilt vessels, hail from the South Sulawesi area of Ujung Pandang, better known to history as Makassar. They continue to play a key role in inter-island trade bringing lumber and other cargo from the outer islands to Jakarta to be exchanged for manufactured goods like cement, flour, tons of rubber sandals and such. Watch for the interesting pay system whereby a laborer gets a small stick for each of the loads he carries across the swaying gangplank which he can later cash in. Just nod to the captain to indicate you would like to board. He will probably give you a cook's tour. If you have lots of time on your hands and a yen for adventure, you can negotiate your services or a fare for a once-in-a-lifetime ride with the Bugis to some of the world's most pristine and exotic islands.

**SUKUR,** a man with a clear vision of the future waits for you in a small Chinese pagoda cluttered with burning incense, religious statuary and ornaments. He reads your fortune from playing cards using an ancient Chinese formula. His fee is at your discretion. At Jalan Budi, Jembatan Dua RT9 RW 4. Bring a translator.

**MISS TJITJIH'S THEATER** features slapstick comedy performances with West Javanese musical accompaniment and attracts Indonesians from all walks of life, from *becak* drivers to businessmen. In days gone by, even Dutch officials came for an unusual night of entertainment. Located in Pasar Angke on Jalan Tubagus in West Jakarta, the theater was established in 1928 by Miss Tjitjih's mother. Besides being a noted dramatist, she was a *pesinden*, one of the women vocalists who sing with Indonesia's lilting gamelan orchestras. The simple building in which the 700-seat theater is located doubles as home for the 27 families involved in the productions. The shows include folk stories, songs and comedy and it is not necessary to understand the language to enjoy them. Performances are held once each evening from 8 to 11. Tickets are only Rp400 each. Miss Tjitjih has been talking of packing up and moving to another location at Jelambar, also in West Jakarta.

**AT THE FROG MARKET** in Jatinegara, five merchants do hopping good business selling thousands of the creatures every day. A controversy over the question of whether Muslims should be allowed to eat frog meat (Islam considers the consumption of frog, *makruh*, to be avoided; pork is *haram*, taboo) was settled when the Indonesian Council of Ulemas, Islamic religious leaders, decided that Muslims were permitted to raise frogs but were not allowed to eat them. A crate of 70 small frogs goes for only Rp2,500. Half crates are available for those with smaller appetites. The frogs are brought in by "hunters" who comb fields and swamps all over the city and in the suburbs. The best time for frog collecting, according to the experts, is sunset when they crank up their throats and croak their mating calls. Tell the taxi driver to take you to Pasar Kodok. Then listen for croaking sounds.

**FOR PUPPET PERFORMANCES** try the Wayang Museum across from the old City Hall (Jakarta City Museum) in Old Batavia on Sunday mornings at 10 a.m. All night performances (the traditional way to watch them) of *Wayang Kulit* (shadow puppets) are staged on the second and last Saturday night of each month in the courtyard of the National Museum on Medan Merdeka.

**NEED A WEEKEND LOVERS HIDEWAY?** Rent a cheap hotel room at Pelabuhan Ratu, a waveswept beach on Java's rugged south coast, a three hour drive about 150 kilometers south of Jakarta. Buy fish at the morning market and choose a different little restaurant each meal to prepare their own special recipe for you. Avoid the water. The currents are too treacherous for swimming and have claimed the lives of unsuspecting visitors. Rehydrate your body after long exposure to the rushing tropical sea winds and sun with a Bir Bintang, Indonesia's excellent premium beer.

**THE SKULLS OF PREHISTORIC JAVA MAN** are kept in a back room of the National Museum. These world-famous fossils were discovered buried in the banks of the Trinil River just outside the Central Java city of Solo after five years of digging by a young Dutch military surgeon named Marie Eugene François Thomas Dubois in 1892. They were one of history's first major anthropological finds and at that time convinced some scholars that Java was the cradle of civilization. Inspired by its beauty, some thinkers speculated Java must have been the site of the Garden of Eden. Dubois' tedious search for evidence of prehistoric man was prompted by the exhaustive work of Alfred Russel Wallace, a British naturalist whose eight years of exploration of the Indonesian archipelago led him to develop a theory of evolution independent of Charles Darwin, but jointly announced by the pair in 1858. Dubois' remarkable find lent further credence to the theories of Wallace and Darwin. He called the skulls and skeletal remains he discovered *Pithecanthropus erectus*, because the creature walked upright. Java Man, as Dubois' skulls became popularly known, lived more than half a million years ago.

**OLD TOMBSTONES** of the founders of Batavia can be examined in Taman Prasasti Cemetery, usually overlooked by tourists, although easily entered east of the Merdeka Palace from Jalan Tanah Abang I. Some of the tombstones were moved here from an ancient church in the center of Old Batavia early last century and bear the inscription H K, which stands for *Hollandsche Kerk* or Dutch Church, their original resting grounds. Notables whose gravestones are here include Jonathan Michiels, reputed to be Batavia's wealthiest landowner ever; Pieter Janse van Hoorn and Sara Bessels, parents of Governor-General John van Hoorn; and, Olivia Miriamme, the first wife of Thomas Stamford Raffles. Consult A. Heuken's *Historical Sites of Jakarta*, for an excellent, detailed account of the cemetery's graves and tombstones. Tombstone buffs will find more fascinating epitaphs and markers at the Wayang Museum.

**THE OLDEST CHURCH** still standing in Jakarta is the Portuguese Church outide the City Walls (so-called because it was built outside the fortress-like compound of Old Batavia) on Jalan Pangeran Jayakarta I. The church, still in use, is now called *Gereja Sion*. It was built between 1693–95 by the Dutch for the multi-racial descendants of the brief Portuguese reign from plans drawn up by Ewout Verhagen, a Rotterdam architect. The church proved to be very popular during the 17th century because it was located on a road famous for its rich country houses surrounded by lush tropical gardens. The interior contains many fine pieces of old furniture, including a Baroque pulpit crafted in 1695.

**RIDE ON A *DELMAN*** through the colorful, bustling streets of Pal Merah in West Jakarta or Kebayoran Lama, South Jakarta. A *delman* is a two-wheeled, horse-drawn carriage, covered with a hood to protect the driver and passengers from rain and prevailing tropical heat.

**MARUNDA,** a fishing village on the north coast of Jakarta, is the site of a restored house reputed to have been the haunt of Si Pitung, a pirate whom local legends have made out to be a kind of 18th century Robin Hood of the area. Simply follow the coastal road (the increasingly narrow road east of Tanjung Priok) to its end, then look beyond the squatters' huts on the beach and the simple plaited bamboo dwellings of the fishermen, for a chocolate-colored stilt house in the distance. Fishermen will be happy to take you across the mouth of the Cakung River for a small fee. Not far from the Si Pitung house is a very old mosque, *Mesjid Alam*. Silt from the river here has yielded many important archaeological treasures including ancient ceramics dating back nearly 2,000 years to the time of the area's earliest Chinese visitors. Marunda is reputedly the spot where Sultan Agung landed his forces in 1628 in an attempt to reclaim the area from the Dutch. Raffles also is said to have first come ashore on Java here with his armada in 1811 when he seized Batavia. It is also the home of one of Jakarta's most popular seafood dishes, *Ikan Bandeng*, and a good spot to catch *Kucing Air*, catfish.

**CILINCING,** on the road to Marunda, is the site of an interesting old Chinese temple or *klenteng* with the name Wan Lin Chie painted on the front and Sam Nyan Kiong painted above the gate. Carved lions guard the entrances. Across from the temple is a footpath to an old mosque which residents say was founded by one of the first missionaries to bring Islam to the islands.

**PASAR MINGGU** offers the chance to enjoy late night dining at food stalls while watching farmers unload tons of fresh produce for Jakarta's morning markets. Easy to get to by taxi.

**VISIT A BATIK FACTORY.** Ibu Bintang Negara's factory demonstrates the process of producing batik from waxing to dyeing in surroundings much like those found in Central Java. The factory is at Jalan Bendungan Hilir 2, Gunung Harli, Senayan, not far from the sprawling Jakarta Hilton Hotel.

**AT THE RATTAN HOUSE,** Jalan Bangka Raya 9A, Kemang, visitors can watch how rattan is woven into custom-made furniture.

**SENAYAN SPORTS COMPLEX** provides a pleasant setting for jogging. Sprays of beautiful orchids are for sale at the Orchid Gardens in the center of the complex. Follow your workout with a

cold beer poolside at the neighboring Hilton Hotel which has a comprehensive jogging layout of its own with marked stops for calisthenics.

**CROCODILE WRESTLING** with a difference. See men who allegedly employ magic powers in the battle against the giant reptiles. Lots of wrestling matches are given on busy Sundays at the Indonesian Jaya Crocodile Farm, Jalan Badengan Utara 27 in Kota on the road to Pluit. Rp1,000 per person admission. It is also a good place to buy local snake, lizard and crocodile skin shoes and handbags.

**THE WORLD'S ONLY REAL DRAGONS** occupy one of the open pens at the highly-recommended Rangunan Zoo, Jalan Rangunan, Pasar Minggu. The Komodo dragons hail from the tiny Indonesian island of the same name between Sumbawa and Flores. These last survivors of the dinosaur age grow up to three meters long, weigh up to 150 kilograms, and have a fire-yellow, forked tongue that drips toxic saliva. The carnivorous lizards are reputed to have devoured a European tourist who visited their island. Many other exotic birds, animals and plants of Indonesia are also on display at the zoo. Open daily from 8 a.m. to 6 p.m.

**THE JAVANESE DANCE DRAMA** at the Bharata Theatre, Jalan Pasar Senen 15, an interesting evening. The theater presents *Wayang Orang* (stories of the Hindu epics, the Mahabarata and Ramayana) and *Ketoprak* (skits based on legends and history) nightly except Saturdays at 8 p.m.

**OLD BANTEN,** the ancient pepper port that preceded Jakarta in importance as an international trading hub up until the 16th century, is a fascinating day trip particularly for those interested in historical sites. Located about 150 kilometers west of Jakarta, it can be reached by car in about two hours, (part of the drive is on expressways). An impressive restoration effort here has recreated some of the port's ancient structures and gathered period pottery, tools and other archaeological finds in a museum. Banten's most impressive building is *Mesjid Agung*, which dates back to 1559. There is also an old watchtower, all that remains of the 17th century Dutch Fort Speelwijk, and the arched walls from an ancient palace that was the residence of the mother of Banten's last sultan. A huge Chinese festival is held each summer at the Wan De Yuan temple, not far from the mosque. Thousands of Chinese pilgrims from Indonesia and other countries flock to pray, burn incense sticks, dine and socialize during the holiday.

**CARITA BEACH AND KRAKATAU VOLCANO.** If you wish to overnight on a lovely beach after visiting Banten, continue driving about an hour west beyond Banten on the road that hugs the coast to Hotel Krakatau on Carita Beach. It offers a range of accommodation from simple bungalows to more expensive air-conditioned bungalows with bathtubs and hot water, and roomy enough for families or groups. Looming in the seas offshore are the remnants of the world-famous Krakatau volcano, which erupted in one of history's most violent explosions in 1883. Day trips to the volcano can be arranged with fishermen in nearby Labuan, but the boats are usually in questionable condition and the ride is long and can be risky. Hotel reservations should be made before leaving Jakarta, especially on weekends, at the Hotel Krakatau's office above the Hotel Menteng's Hero Supermarket, Jalan Gondangdia Lama 28, (Tel. 330–846).

**TAMAN ISMAIL MARZUKI,** just east of Menteng at Jalan Cikini Raya 73, (Tel. 322–606) is Jakarta's arts and culture center. TIM, as it is known, has an almost perpetual schedule of traditional and contemporary Indonesian performing arts including dance, drama and music, painting and handicraft exhibitions, literary readings and cinema, as well as occasional performances by visiting dance, drama and music troupes from the West in its open air and indoor theaters and exhibition halls. It is well worth a visit if just to soak up some of the atmosphere of the city's creative life. There is also a Planetarium which has English-language shows (Tel. 337–530).

**PULAU SERIBU,** the "Thousand Islands" (actually only 112) in the Java Sea north of Jakarta, offers the best beaches, snorkeling, diving and other typical tropical island activities near the city. The easiest way to arrange a trip to the islands is P.T. Pulau Seribu Paradise, in the Jakarta Theater Building on Jalan Thamrin (Tel. 359–333/4) which provides transportation by plane (around U.S.$120 per person plus tax for the daily 25 minutes flight) or boat (U.S.$50 for the 2 to 3 hour trip), accommodation (U.S.$30 to $120 per bungalow depending on size, amenities and island), meals and water-sports gear. The agent offers all-inclusive packages which run from U.S.$80 to U.S.$300 per person excluding transport for two to six nights. The Pulau Papa Theo dive camp offers packages especially tailored for divers from U.S.$66 to U.S.$216 per person. In addition to the alluring white sand and azure seas there are excellent coral gardens off the islands of Genting, Opak Besar and Putri. Others, like Onrust, Kelor and Kahyangan have ruins which are of historical interest for the role they played in the development of Jakarta. Weekends are crowded and more expensive.

**TUGU,** a small settlement south of Tanjung Priok, still exudes some of the flavor of Jakarta's first Western immigrants, the Portuguese, even though it has been nearly 500 years since they made only a brief appearance here.

# Best Bets

**SUNNY AFTERNOON DELIGHT.** Try splashing around in the giant swimming pool complex at Taman Impian Jaya Ancol (Dreamland) on Jakarta Bay. It has maxi-water shoots, wave-making machines, white water rapids, water spouts and giant slides. Open 6 a.m. to 10 p.m. Saturday, Sundays and public holidays and from 8 a.m. to 10 p.m. on other days. Before or after swimming, watch how real fish do it at the dolphin and sea lion show in the adjoining Gelanggan Samudra complex. (Tel. 680–519 or 681–057).

**FRESH OYSTERS, LIVE SHRIMP AND MUSSELS** for a delicious Sunday afternoon *paella* party can be bought at Pasar Muara Karang, near Pluit, in north Jakarta.

**STONES** from Pelangi's shop, which specializes in black and white opals, natural and cultured pearls, and gems that are reputed to bring good luck. Available at the Indonesian Bazaar, Shop 37, Jakarta Hilton Hotel and Pasar Ular, North Jakarta, open 9 a.m. to 8 p.m.

**DISCOS.** The best social discourse at a disco at the venerable Tanamur, Jalan Tanah Abang Timur 14 (Tel. 353–947). Elbow your way through the crowds at Stardust, arguably Southeast Asia's largest, Jayakarta Tower Hotel, Jalan Hayam Wuruk 126 (Tel. 624–408). Enjoy an elegant evening at the expensive Ebony, Kuningan Plaza, Jalan Rasuna Said (Tel. 513–700).

**CASSETTES,** inexpensive and high quality, can be purchased from the enormous, wall-to-wall selection of tapes at Duta Suara (Tel. 325–471). It is technically at Jalan H. Agus Salim 26A, but taxi drivers only respond if you tell them "Jalan Sabang". Sample the cassettes on the banks of decks and headphones in air-conditioned comfort. Buy eight cassettes, Rp1,700 to 2,000 each, and get a free carrying case.

**POPULAR PUBS** include the George and Dragon, Jalan Teluk Betung 32 (Tel. 325–625) where the fixtures include dart boards and Rugby Club members; the Jaya Pub on Jalan M.H. Thamrin across from the Sari Pacific Hotel and up the stairs behind the Jaya Building features live jazz by superb Indonesian singers and combos.

**MOST COMPREHENSIVE MAP** of Jakarta is the Falk Plan Map, available from major hotel shops and bookstores for about Rp7,000. It may be too detailed for the casual, short-term visitor.

**RELIABLE TAXI SERVICE** is Bluebird. Call 325–607 for 24-hour radio service and bookings.

**ENJOY INDONESIAN CAMARADERIE** by circling the base of the National Monument with joggers at dawn or early on Sunday when main streets are closed to traffic and entire families spill into the street for recreation.

**ANTIQUE STALLS.** The longest stretch is on Jalan Surabaya in Menteng. Novices shop here at their own risk as many items are "instant" antiques. It can, however, turn up some good buys.

**MIDNIGHT SNACK** especially good after dancing at the Tanamur Disco: *bubur ayam* (chicken soup porridge) at the 24-hour Java Coffee Shop (Tel. 320–008), Hotel Indonesia, where you can also people-watch for relations of Billy Kwan of the movie "Year of Living Dangerously" fame.

**MOST SPECTACULAR VIEW** of Jakarta while snacking on *sushi* is at Yakiniku Duidoman, Korea Tower, 30th Floor, Bank Bumi Daya Building, Jalan Imam Bonjol.

**TROPICAL SUNSET** while sipping a cool drink at the Town House, 15th Floor, Wisma Metropolitan II, Jalan Sudirman. On clear afternoons the restaurant provides a panorama of melting pink and orange clouds before a deep crimson engulfs the volcanic mountain backdrop of the sprawling city.

**RIJSTTAFEL,** the Dutch appellation for "rice table," is served at one of Jakarta's most atmospheric restaurants, the Oasis, a massive old colonial residence with black-and-white flag-tiled floors, tall stained-glass windows and a fascinating collection of paintings, carvings, masks, fetishes, weavings and antiques from throughout the archipelago. Twenty pretty young ladies, each traditionally dressed in a colorful, form-fitting *sarong kebaya*, sashay one by one to your table with a different Indonesian dish. Enthusiastic performances beginning at 9 p.m. by a troupe of Batak singers, debatably the archipelago's best singers, make dining here an event. Open 11:30 a.m. to midnight daily, except Sunday, at Jalan Raden Saleh 47. Reservations recommended. (Tel. 326–397, 327–818).

**BEST-MADE AND UNUSUAL FABRICS,** including cotton and silk batik and woven *ikat*, in a variety of contemporary and traditional designs, is at Iwan Tirta, Jalan Panarukan 25 (Tel. 349–122), and the Borobudur Intercontinental. Also try Danar Hadi, Jalan Raden Saleh 1A (Tel. 342–390).

**PRACTICAL BOOKS FOR NEWCOMERS** are *Introducing Indonesia* (Rp15,000) and, to get acquainted with "open-air shopping", *A Jakarta Market* (Rp5,000) by Kaarin Wall. Both are published by the American Women's Association (Tel.773–154) which donates profits from the sale of the books to charitable projects.

**HANDICRAFTS ARE CREATED BEFORE YOUR EYES** at the pleasant, outdoor Pasar Seni Art Market at Ancol Dreamland. Indoors, Sarinah Department Store on Jalan Thamrin (3rd Floor) and at Blok M also have a large selection.

**ATMOSPHERE FOR TENNIS** is at the Hotel Borobudur courts which are set amid lush tropical

gardens. The hotel also offers the city's biggest swimming pool and ballroom.

**OUT-OF-TOWN TRIP** within a two hour drive is Bogor with its world-famous botanical gardens, palace and vistas of tea plantations and volcanos.

**AMERICAN-STYLE SUPERMARKET** is Kem Chiks, Jalan Kemang Raya 3 (Tel. 798–8085) open 8:30 a.m.–7:30 daily, except Sundays 9–1.

**CHEAP, FUNKY T-SHIRTS** can be found at Matahari Department Store in Ratu Plaza, Jalan Sudirman.

**PLACE FOR PHOTOGRAPHING MOSQUE ACTIVITIES** is from the tiers of balconies on three sides of the massive prayer hall of the Istiqlal Mosque on Merdeka Square. Avoid the rear of the second tier because it has the control booth for the lights and microphones. The fifth floor balcony is an awe-inspiring place to hear the chant — in unison — of thousands, reverberating through the mosque.

**EAT A SUPER KING-SIZED MEATBALL,** *Bakso Bola "tenis"* prepared from special East Javanese recipe at Pondok Remaja, Jalan Wijaya, Kebayoran Baru open 9 a.m. to 10 p.m. daily.

**GUIDE TO INDONESIAN CUISINE** presented in a cultural context is *Selera* magazine. Published monthly, it sells out quickly. In Indonesian with an English language supplement.

**PENTHOUSE** is on top of the Garden Tower at the city's best hotel, the Jakarta Hilton, Jalan Jenderal Gatot Subroto (Tel. 583–041, 587–981). It has its own private swimming pool overlooking the city and the hotel's 13 hectares of exquisitely-landscaped gardens and facilities, service elevator and helicopter pad. The rooms are elegantly decorated with fabrics, paintings and art works representing various islands. The round tub in the master bathroom is almost large enough to swim laps in and has 24-karat gold fixtures. At U.S.$2,000 per night plus tax and service, the penthouse also has the most impressive price tag in town if not all Asia.

**BUYS ON FLUTED PILLARS,** the architectural rage for new homes in Jakarta's exclusive residential districts, are along Jalan Gatot Subroto in the Cawang area, East Jakarta and down Slipi up to Grogol, east of the Hilton Hotel. Take home a touch of ancient Greece or Rome for just Rp50,000 to 100,000 per pillar.

**INGREDIENTS FOR HOLDING THE WORLD'S GREATEST STINK PARTY** are *durian*, the king of Indonesian fruits, famed for smelling like rotten onions in an outhouse; *pete*, beans with their own pungent oil; *ikan asin*, salted, dried fish; and, *jengkol*, another magic bean. Fry *terasi*, a popular, fermented shrimp, as guests arrive. Advisable to skip work and socializing the following day.

**PHOTOCOPYING SERVICES** galore are lined up on the streets in front of the Hotel Hyatt. Rp25 per page. Book-binding is available.

**GUIDE TO THE ARCHITECTURE** and antiquities of old Jakarta is *Historical Sites of Jakarta* by Father A. Heuken SJ, Cipta Loka Caraka: 1982. Available at hotels and bookstores.

**PANORAMIC CITY VIEW** from the top of the National Monument which can be reached either by lift or elevator, depending on whether you hail from Australia or the U.S.

**SINGING FEATHERED FRIENDS** can be bought at one of the 84 stalls at the bird market, Pasar Burung, on Kramat Pela, Jalan Barito, Kebayoran Baru. Talk to Pak Amat who has sold birds there for 15 years, and ask to see his Falk Parrot from Australia (Rp45,000). If you can train a *Mei Hwa* from China (Rp75,000 per pair), the value of the birds soars from Rp150,000 to Rp300,000. Colorful local species include *Kuitlang*, *Beo*, *Tekukur*, *Gelatik*, and *Kacamata*.

**SCHEDULE OF CITY EVENTS,** including cultural performances, lectures and exhibitions, is the "Where to Go" section of the *Jakarta Post*.

**HALF-HOUR LOOK AT INDONESIA** is the spectacular Imax film at *Keong Mas*, the Golden Snail Theatre at Taman Mini Indonesia. Screened at noon, 2 and 4 p.m. daily, Rp2,000. Avoid Sundays as the crowds are very large.

**WARUNGS (FOOD STALLS)** open after sunset along Jalan Mangga Besar. Sample the *Kway Tiow Medan*, Sumatran fried noodles, and *Kueh Basah*, Jakarta's famous steamed rice cakes in a rainbow of colors. Also in the parking lot of Sarinah on Jalan Thamrin. The best seafood found in food stalls is served along Jalan Peconongan, near Pasar Bahru, Central Jakarta.

**ADVICE FOR HEALTH MAINTENANCE** is in "Staying Healthy in Indonesia," produced by the American Women's Association (Tel. 773–154) and the International Allied Medical Association.

**SELECTION OF EUROPEAN BREADS AND PASTRIES,** including Mother Earth whole wheat health loaves, at Vineth Bakery, Jalan Panglima Polim and at Kem Chicks in Kemang.

**FRIED DUMPLINGS** cooked on a thick cast iron griddle over a bed of red coals at the Rumah Makan Sedap, Jalan Gunung Sehari I, No. 19. Raucous atmosphere. Check out the calendars on the walls.

**COIFFURES** From the elegant to the outrageous, whipped up at Alexander Daniel's (management from the well-known Rudy Hadisuwarno's salons.) Full-service available. Jalan Jambu 41 (Tel. 325–041). Good stop on a steamy day.

**MEN'S HAIRCUTS AND STYLING** at Sarawita, Jakarta Hilton Hotel. Masjud is particularly good. Only Rp6,000 so do tip.

SEAFOOD is at Jun Nyan, Jalan Batu Ceper 69 (Tel. 364–063) or Nelayan Seafood Market and Restaurant in the old Jai-Alai fronton at Ancol Dreamland (Tel. 680–108).

DUTCH ORGAN MUSIC and visions of Old Batavia are at Club Noordwijk Restaurant, Jalan Juanda 5A Tel. 353–909.

JAZZ is at the Captains Bar in the Jakarta Mandarin Hotel (Tel. 321–307). The Funk Section plays Monday through Saturday evenings.

BOOKSTORE is Gunung Agung, which is also Jakarta's oldest and largest, at Jalan Kwitang (Tel. 354–563) and Ratu Plaza, Jalan Sudirman (Tel. 734–648).

PARADE OF FASHION by some of Indonesia's most stunning models wearing the creations of Jakarta's leading, and most inventive, designers. Held every Friday at lunchtime over buffet lunch at Pete's Club, a restaurant operated by Rima Melati, herself a film star and model, Gunung Sewu, Jalan Gatot Subroto, Kav. 22 (Tel. 515-478).

JAVANESE-ARAB FOOD is the *nasi kebuli* ("rice dish") at Restaurant Srivijaya, Hotel Srivijaya, Jalan Veteran 1 (Tel. 370–409).

COUNTRY-WESTERN MUSIC at the Green Pub in the Jakarta Theater Building, Jalan Thamrin (Tel. 359–332) on Fridays until closing. Until 9:30 pm other nights. Featuring Tex-Mex food and great salsa picante.

KINDERGARTEN READINESS PROGRAM is the Kartini Play Group directed by Georgette Haskin, (Tel. 772–325).

MOST APTLY NAMED NIGHT SPOT is the Hotmen Bar, Hotel Menteng I, Jalan Gondangdia Lama 28 (Tel. 325–208). Long a favorite haunt of

"oilies," its name is merely an abbreviated version of the hotel's, but the double entendre tells you exactly what goes on here. Attracts self-employed young women but transactions with them are strictly at your own risk.

TRADITIONAL TEXTILES in a 19th century mansion is in the Textile Museum on Jalan Satsuit. About 600 different kinds of Indonesian textiles are on display from batiks from all over Indonesia and double ikat from the Lesser Sundas to Dayak bark cloths from Borneo. Clothing serves important social functions and is also closely connected with religious practices.

FRIED CHICKEN, a passion in Indonesia as well as in America, is the Central Javanese recipe served up at *Ayam Goreng Mbok Berek*, Jalan Panglima Polim Raya 105 and Jalan Prof. Dr. Soepomo 2, Tebet (Tel. 829–5366).

BETAWI SATAY *kambing*, marinated bits of lamb skewered on a stick and cooked over coals from the *warung* in front of BNI 46, Jalan Kebon Sirih. The stall smells heavily of goat, but the satay is divine.

HI-TECH AMUSEMENT THEME PARK IN SOUTHEAST ASIA and the only Disneyland-style center in the region is *Dunia Fantasie*, Fantasy World, (Tel. 682–417, 683–616) at Ancol Dreamland. Watch the electronic monkeys perform in the *Teater Kera Balada Kera* and the expressions on the faces of the Indonesian children and adults. Even if you do not understand the Indonesian language wisecracks and song lyrics the experience is fun. Also try the heart-stopping ride over the crest of the giant *Kincir Raksasa Bianglala* ferris wheel. Open Monday through Fridays 3 p.m. to 10 and Saturday, Sundays and public holidays, 10 a.m. to 10 p.m.

CLUB for expatriate wives who want to learn about Indonesian culture is the Ganesha Volunteers, National Museum (Tel. 360–551).

PADANG food, the hot and spicy kind from West Sumatra, is at *Sari Bundo*, Jalan Ir. H. Juanda 27 (Tel. 358–343). The *rendang*, a rich meat curry, is especially good.

TRADITIONAL JAVANESE MASSAGE or *pijat* in the local lingo is offered at the Anna Health Centre, Cikini Sofyan Hotel, Jalan Cikini Raya 79 (Tel. 320–695 ext. 44). Rp10,500 per hour includes room with steam box. Use of fitness equipment is Rp2,500 additional.

METHOD OF GETTING RID OF 'MASUK ANGIN' ("The Wind Enters") — the town's most talked about ailment that is caused by drafts from light winds, air-conditioning, electric fans, open car windows, etc — is Massage Rheumason, a hot mentholated cream, into the problem area by rapidly rubbing the skin with the side of a Rp100 coin. It is a painful but interesting experience.

## Travel Notes

### Land and People

Jakarta is the capital of the Republic of Indonesia, a vast nation of 13,677 islands that straddles the equator for more than 5,120 kilometers from west to east. The city covers 650 square kilometers of the northwest corner of Indonesia's historical and cultural nexus, the island of Java, at a southern latitude of 6 degrees 17 minutes and an eastern longitude of 106 degrees 17 minutes.

About seven million of Indonesia's estimated 165 million people crowd densely-populated Jakarta with both figures increasing rapidly. Indonesians who hail from almost every part of the diverse archipelago have brought a vibrant mix of cultures from their islands to their beloved *Ibukota*, mother city. About 90 per cent of all Indonesians are Muslims, but the government, which rules Indonesia from Jakarta through a parliamentary democracy, guarantees the right of worship for Christians, Hindus and Buddhists alike.

### Getting There and Getting Around

#### By Air

Many major international airlines fly to Jakarta, most via Singapore, the small, independent island nation to the northwest. Air passengers arrive at the Soekarno-Hatta International Airport located on the coastal plains near Cengkareng, 23 kilometers west of Jakarta. Regular flights of about an hour-and-a-half shuttle back-and-forth between Singapore and Jakarta throughout the day. Indonesia's national carrier, Garuda, and Singapore Airlines offer one-month excursion fares for around U.S.$200 round trip. Garuda and several other regional carriers offer direct flights to Jakarta from Hong Kong, Tokyo, and Australia.

Visitors wishing to explore other parts of the vast archipelago after seeing Jakarta should inquire about Garuda's VIP, the Visit Indonesia Pass. It enables passengers to visit up to five cities for U.S.$300, ten for $400 and a phenomenal 33 cities in any of the islands for U.S.$500 but can only be purchased with an international round trip ticket bought in the United States, Europe, Japan, Australia and New Zealand. The VIP pass is not available in Singapore. For domestic flight information call Garuda Indonesia, (Tel. 370–709), Jalan Ir. H. Juanda 15, or one of its branches.

#### By Sea

Ships arriving in Jakarta dock at Tanjung Priok Harbor, 10 kilometers east of the city center. A number of luxury liners from foreign ports make regular calls. For details of their schedules, contact Setia Tours, Jalan Pinangsia Raya, Glodok Plaza, Blok B, No. 1. Jakarta; (Tel. 630–008). Write them at P.O. Box 1104, Jakarta Kota. Telex. 41290.

The government's Pelni Lines (Jalan Pintu Air 1, (Tel. 358–398) offers a most relaxing opportunity to get to other parts of Java and other Indonesian islands by ship. Four large, air-conditioned passenger vessels ply the usually placid, equatorial waters. The price of a comfortable first- or second-class cabin, equipped with private bathroom, color television, videos and three meals a day is less than that of an air ticket between the same points. Book passage through a travel agent.

### By Rail

There are five major train stations in the city. Most of the trains running from Kota Station, near Old Batavia, connect Jakarta with points in Central and East Java. The Bima train has sleeping compartments for its overnight express runs to Yogyakarta and Solo. Trains from Gambir Station on the eastern flank of Merdeka Square make short trips to Bogor and Bandung.

The best place to purchase train tickets is from Carnation Travel Agency, Jalan Menteng Raya 24 one block from the Hyatt Hotel, (Tel. 344–027, 356–728), and at Jalan Kyai Maja 53, Kebayoran Baru, (Tel. 713–943). Tickets can be purchased at the station during the morning of the day of departure and most trains leave in the afternoon.

### By Bus

Several reputable companies offer passage on air-conditioned coaches to other parts of Java and to Bali and Sumatra via ferry crossings. Ask a travel agent for details.

### Weather

Situated along the equator, Jakarta has weather that is almost always sunny, hot and muggy. There are only two main seasons. The wet season occurs from November to April; the dry from May to October, give or take a month. Average annual rainfall is around one meter. Jakarta's average temperature is 27°C (81°F) during the day and 25°C (77°F) at night. That may seem moderate, but the average humidity, a soggy 81 per cent, may make it seem hotter. Balmy breezes that accompany the beautiful sunsets provide some relief. The best time to bathe, or *mandi*, is at sunset when your body is fully aware of the subtle temperature changes. Some people prefer to visit during the rainy season when sporadic torrential downpours clear the dust and smog from the late afternoon skies.

### Customs and Entry Rules

All travelers to Indonesia must possess passports valid for at least six months from the day of arrival and a return or through air ticket. Nationals from 28

countries including the U.S., Australia, New Zealand and most non-communist European and Asian countries receive automatic tourist visa chops upon arrival that permit them to remain in Indonesia for up to two months, but extensions are not permitted. However entry by air or sea through ports other than Jakarta, Surabaya, Bali, Medan, Manado, Biak, Ambon, Batam and Pekanbaru requires a valid visa prior to arrival. Visas for a period of up to 30 days, extendable up to three months, can be obtained from any Indonesian Embassy or overseas consulate. Business visas must also be obtained overseas prior to arrival. A *surat jalan,* a police permit, may be required for travel to some remote areas of the country. In Jakarta they can be obtained at Police Headquarters (Markas Besar Kepolisian Republik Indonesia), Jalan Trunojoyo, Kebayoran Baru.

A maximum of two liters of alcoholic beverages, 200 cigarettes, 50 cigars or 100 grams of tobacco and a reasonable amount of perfume for personal use may be brought into Indonesia exempt from duty. Camera equipment, typewriters, radios and automobiles may be brought in provided visitors leave with them, but they must be declared at Customs.

Pornography, television sets, radios and cassette recorders, printed matter in Chinese characters and Chinese medicines are prohibited. Penalties for bringing in narcotics are very severe.

There is no restriction on the import or export of foreign currencies and travelers checks, but the import or export of more than Rp50,000 is illegal.

## Airport Information

The Melati Bhakti Duty Free Shop is located at the top of the escalator just beyond passport control. After clearing immigration and customs, swarms of luggage porters and taxi drivers will descend on you. They should be tipped Rp300–500 per bag depending on its size. Most major hotels send vehicles to meet their guests and the charge will be added to your bill. Metered taxis, some of them air-conditioned, cost about Rp13,000 plus the tollway fee of Rp2,700. A surcharge of Rp2,300 is also added to the registered meter fare on trips originating at the airport only road. Bluebird taxis offer a 50 per cent discount on toll charges on trips to or from the airport.

The airport authority also operates an air-conditioned bus service to and from five points in the city every 20 minutes. The fare is Rp2,000 per passenger including luggage. An expressway connects Soekarno-Hatta International Airport with Jakarta, but allow 45 minutes for travel to destinations in the city where traffic jams are common.

There is an airport tax of Rp9,000 for passengers departing on international flights, Rp2,000 for domestic flights.

## Health

Valid international certificates for smallpox, cholera and yellow fever vaccinations are required only for travelers coming from infected areas. Typhoid, paratyphoid· and cholera vaccinations, though not required, are advisable, especially for those continuing on from Jakarta to other parts of the country. Malaria prophylactic tablets (Fansidar and Choloroquin) are strongly recommended for use in many non-urban areas. Gammaglobulin shots will help reduce the impact of hepatitis, if not prevent it.

Bouts of diarrhoea are common, not necessarily because of unhygienic conditions, but because of the drastic changes in climate and cuisine. Newcomers should eat sparingly but drink plenty of tea and other liquids. Go easy on the chili peppers that spice up many Indonesian dishes. It is not safe to drink water directly from the tap. All drinking water must be boiled for at least 10 minutes. A variety of bottled waters (Aqua, Oasis, Vit) are readily available in many provision shops.

Raw vegetables can also cause stomach problems and should be avoided except in some of the international hotels (the Hotel Borobudur has a luscious salad bar). After a crash course in Advanced Diarrhoea, the stomach should become more tolerant to more daring dining adventures.

The tropical sun can be deceptively intense, even on cloudy days. Use high-powered sun screens and tanning lotions and drink plenty of liquids while touring the city. Overexposure and dehydration can be devastating.

For routine medical care, try The Medical Scheme, Setiabudi Building, Jalan H. Rasuna Said, Kuningan, (Tel. 515–367, manned 24 hours, and 515-597 during office hours). It is a private membership group but will take non-members upon referral and in the event of emergency. Another alternative is the Metropolitan Medical Center, Wisata Office Tower, west of Hotel Indonesia, Tel. 320–408 which also has some capable dentists. Two well-stocked pharmacies are: Apotik Melawai, Jalan Melawai Raya 191, Kebayoran, Tel. 716–109; and, Apotik Senayan, Jalan Pakubuwono VI/6, Kebayoran Baru, Tel. 715–821. Both are open daily.

### What to Wear

Dress is usually casual in Jakarta. Airy cotton clothes will not prevent sweating, but they tend to be more comfortable in the sticky city heat.

Women should dress modestly out of respect for the Muslims. Avoid wearing skimpy sundresses and

short pants in public. In other words, women's wear is basically the same as it is in any major Western city in the west — "smart casual".

For men making business calls, a short-sleeved shirt and tie should suffice. Even more comfortable and acceptable in Jakarta (but considered passe in neighboring Singapore) are safari-style leisure suits which enable you to leave ties in your luggage. A long-sleeved batik shirt, worn open-neck (and never tucked in) over dark trousers, is *de rigueur* evening attire for men. Cool batik dresses in very fashionable patterns and styles make smart, comfortable women's evening wear.

Sweaters, shawls or light jackets may be needed for jaunts to outlying mountain areas or even in hotel reception halls and some restaurants that have been transformed into walk-in refrigerators by the air-conditioning. Very casual beach wear is in bad taste anywhere but on a beach. An umbrella also comes in handy both as a sunshade and in the event of a tropical downpour.

## Money

Bank Bumi Daya operates a currency exchange near the luggage claim area of the airport, but major transactions should be conducted with money changers in the city which offer better foreign exchange rates for currency and travelers checks. P.T. Sinar Iriawan (in Menteng behind the President Hotel on Jalan Irian 3, (Tel. 352–643, 351–115) gives friendly service as well as good rates. Or try Ayumas Gunung Agung, Jalan Kwitang 24–26, (Tel. 349–490 and 342–944).

The local currency is called rupiah (not rupee as in India) and is hard to handle. Even if you have a full complement of bills, they will never seem to be large enough — or small enough. The largest denomination is Rp10,000, but don't let all the zeros throw you. That is the equivalent of substantially less than U.S.$10 (the 1986 devaluation brought the value of the rupiah down to around Rp1,630 to the U.S. dollar.) So for major transactions at banks and money changers, you will need to carry one briefcase just for the bills. Travelers checks (U.S. dollars preferred) and major credit cards are accepted at airline offices, the big hotels, many restaurants and big shops. But most stores and small establishments seldom accept currency other than rupiah.

When changing money make sure to ask for plenty of Rp1,000 and 500 notes as taxi drivers and others dealing in small bills routinely claim they do not have change for 10,000 or even 5,000 — even when they do. Most banks are open from 8 a.m. to noon Monday through Friday and 8 a.m. to 11 a.m. on Saturdays.

## Tipping

Most hotels and their restaurants add a service charge of 10 per cent to the bill (on top of the government tax of 11 per cent). In other restaurants where there is no service charge, a tip of five to 10 per cent is appropriate, depending on the service and the type of establishment, but is not mandatory.

## Bargaining

Many of the modern shopping complexes, supermarkets and department stores in Jakarta have fixed prices. But bargaining is customary — indeed almost expected — at small shops, stalls and more traditional marketplaces where even price tags have little meaning. Approach bargaining as a friendly and fun way to socialize with someone you might not otherwise have a chance to chat with and forget about whether you actually are getting a bargain or not. The basic formula is to offer half the asking price, then quit when you reach the maximum price you wish to pay for an item.

## Taxis

Jakarta's ubiquitous yellow, blue and green taxis are the best way of making short trips around the city. They have been upgraded in recent years but many still do not have air-conditioning (or "*ah-say*" as Indonesians call it) and may look like they compete in Demolition Derbies — on the losing side when off-duty. Flagfall is Rp400 without and Rp600 with "*ah-say*" for the first kilometer increasing in increments of Rp200 or Rp270 respectively for each subsequent kilometer. Taxis can easily be hailed by simply waving a hand almost anywhere. Make sure the meter is started after you enter. Tipping is not expected but drivers often claim they have no change so simply let them keep the small stuff. That will win you many friends.

If you plan to make several stops or want your clothes and hair to remain sweat-free, you can rent taxis with air-conditioning at most hotels for as little as Rp7,500 per hour (minimum two hours) or from "taxi-gelap" stands at Jalan Kediri behind the Menteng football field or the carpark next to Kartika Plaza Hotel on Jalan Jenderal Sudirman. Bluebird has the best 24-hour radio-dispatch service (Tel. 325–607).

## Rental Cars and Driving

Renting cars without a driver is not advisable especially for newcomers, but if you insist, Avis (Tel. 370–108) has them for a flat fee of U.S.$100 daily. Its head office is at Jalan Maluku 13 (Tel. 336–942). Hertz head office is at the Jakarta Mandarin Hotel (Tel. 371–208, 321–307). It only rents out its vehicles with drivers at a U.S. $33 minimum for the

first two hours and $16.50 for each additional hour.

The golden rule for drivers in Jakarta is to focus only on what is happening in front of you and try to forget about what is going on beyond the back seat. The steering wheel is on the right side and you drive on the left side of the road. Some streets that have two-way traffic most of the day become one-way at certain busy times. Keep an eye out for the signs near the many roundabouts that indicate when you are not permitted to circumnavigate the circle (usually the better part of the morning rush hours). Be aggressive during the frequent traffic jams or you may be trapped in the same spot for hours.

Watch out for motorcycles (which rarely watch out for automobiles) and for other two-, three-, and four-wheeled vehicles. When stopped by policemen, be polite and you may get off with an instructive, friendly lecture. More cars are stopped for violations just before the Islamic Lebaran holidays. The reason is your guess.

### Buses

Only the most adventurous travelers will want to try getting around Jakarta aboard its legions of jam-packed, smoke-belching public and private buses, minibuses and vans. They are cheap, Rp100 per trip, but usually like saunas inside. The city's public and private buses, minivans, oplets and mikrolets course through a mystifying array of routes and may fly past your stop if you are not paying attention. The Tourist Information Centers may have the latest detailed bus routes.

### Other Interesting Ways of Getting Around

Despite continuing efforts to rid the city of them, Jakarta's famous people-powered trishaws, the *becaks*, can still be found gliding through the side streets, particularly at night when they provide a cool, pleasant, alternative means of transport. They are prohibited from using main thoroughfares during the day. Two forms of motorized trishaws are the *bajaj* or *helicak* and small vans called *bemo* are also popular modes of getting around. Fares for all these vehicles are based on a complicated distance formula (usually whatever the driver can get) or Rp300–500 for short jaunts.

For an old-fashioned afternoon ride, the *delman* or the *dokar* — the horse and buggy — can still be found in some parts of the city. Ask for a one to two hour ride but agree upon a price in advance. Then, sit back and watch the fascinating scenes of life in the Indonesian capital go by to the rhythm of the horse's clickety-clacking feet. Call out *Tolong berhenti* (Please stop!) should you wish to. The driver will probably offer to act as tour guide as well. Negotiate in advance for special service.

### Communications

Public telephones can be found throughout most parts of Jakarta, although they are not always in working order. They hungrily consume one Rp50 coin every three minutes so bring a handful if you have a lot to say.

Most international hotels have direct long-distance dialing, telegram and telex services, but add big service charges. Otherwise international and interlocal calls can be made at the Kantor Telepon in the Skyline Building, Jalan M.H. Thamrin 9; Jayakarta Tower Hotel, Jalan Hayam Wuruk; and at the airport. Telegrams can be sent from Gedung Telekomunikasi, Jalan Merdeka Selatan 12.

For fast, accurate delivery throughout the world contact DHL Courier Service (P.T. Birotika Semesta), Wisma Metropolitan Building II, 8th Floor, Jalan Jenderal Sudirman. Call 579–1616 for pick-up.

### Media

There are three English-language daily newspapers published in Jakarta: the *Jakarta Post*, *Indonesian Observer* and the *Indonesian Times*. The *Jakarta Post* is sometimes sold on the main streets but more easily purchased at the large hotels as are *The Asian Wall Street Journal* and *International Herald Tribune*. Prices sometimes vary.

Television and radio, operated and owned by the government, are almost completely in the Indonesian language. In Jakarta, children's TV programs in English are broadcast at 5:30 pm. and there is an English newscast (local and international) at 6:30 pm. Some hotels have in-house video movies that change each month.

### Language

Bahasa Indonesia is the national language although more than 250 distinct languages and dialects are spoken throughout the archipelago. A compact basic language guide that is available in hotels and bookstores is "How to Master the Indonesian Language" by A.M. Almatsier. Some common bahasa Indonesia words and phrases follow.

*Bapak* — used to address an older man or a male VIP.
*Ibu* — used to address an older woman or a female VIP.
*Nyonya* — used to address a married woman.
*Nona* — used to address an unmarried lady.

| Thank you | *Terima kasih!* |
| Good morning | *Selamat pagi* |
| I want to go to... | *Saya mau pergi ke...* |
| What is the fare? | *Berapa ongkos?* |
| stop! | *berhenti!* |
| driver | *sopir* |

| karcis | ticket |
|--------|--------|
| pelan pelan! | slow down! |
| taksi | taxi |
| lapangan terbang | airport |
| utara | north |
| selatan | south |
| timur | east |
| barat | west |
| dekat | near |
| jauh | far |
| kamar kecil | toilet |
| Saya tidak mengerti | I don't understand |
| Maaf! | Excuse me! |
| ya | yes |
| tidak, bukan | no |
| dilarang | forbidden |
| buka | open |
| tertutup | closed |
| awas! | caution! |
| Saya mau beli... | I want to buy... |
| berapa | how much |
| terlalu mahal | too expensive |
| murah | cheap |
| uang | money |
| teh | tea |
| kopi | coffee |
| air | water |
| minuman | drink |
| makanan | food |
| roti | bread |
| nasi | rice |
| mie | noodles |
| goreng | fried |
| ayam | chicken |
| sapi | beef |
| babi | pork |
| ikan | fish |
| dingin | cold |
| sayuran | vegetable |
| buah-buahan | fruit |

## Thefts

The streets of Jakarta are generally safer than those of most Western cities, but use common sense especially in crowded areas where pickpockets will have no remorse about relieving you of your purse or wallet. Refrain from ostentatious displays of expensive watches and jewelry. Women can travel freely in the city without fear of harassment but should dress modestly to avoid attracting attention. Most parking areas have attendants, either official or self-employed, who will keep on eye on your car for only Rp100–200. If you need the police, call KOMDAK Metro Jaya, Pelayanan Masyarakat, Jalan Sudirman. The telephone, 510–110, is manned 24 hours. Ring again if busy.

## Tours

Pacto Ltd., Indonesia's largest tour operator, offers a variety of trips around Jakarta and to some of the neighboring areas. For details call Pacto's Hotel Borobudur Intercontinental office, Tel. 370–108 or Jalan Surabaya 8, (Tel. 348–634). Also recommended is Nitour, Jalan Majapahit 2, Tel. 346–347. Popular city tours include the historical sites — the old harbor area of Sunda Kelapa and the Taman Fatahillah (center of Old Batavia ) — an Ancol Handicraft Tour, the Jalan Surabaya antique market, Taman Mini Indonesia, the Bogor Botanical Gardens, and Puncak highlands.

Excellent English-language tours of the National Museum are given by the Ganesha Volunteers, a group of expatriate cultural enthusiasts, on Tuesday, Wednesday and Thursday mornings at 9:30 a.m. Tours in French and Japanese can also be arranged according to your schedule.

## Emergencies

Consult the first page of the Jakarta Phone Directory for "Important Numbers" (The number for the Family Planning office is listed immediately after the number to report a fire!)

*Heart attacks:*
Intensive Coronary Care Unit (Cardiac Emergency)
Central Hospital (Rumah Sakit Cipto)
Jl. Diponegoro 71, Menteng
Tel. 344–003 (Emergency Room also)

*For burns and other emergencies:*
Pertamina Hospital
Jl. Kyai Maja 29, Kebayoran
Tel. 707–214, 707–211 (Emergency Room)

If you call a hospital, be prepared to speak Indonesian. All hospitals are clearly marked on the FALK MAP of Jakarta. Bring cash with you to facilitate service.

*24-hour Doctor-on-call Service:*
SOS Medica, Jalan Prapanca Raya 33–34.
Tel. 771–575, 774–198 or 733–094
(If required, a doctor will accompany patient to Pertamina Hospital. Cash fee for service.)

*Ambulances:*
118 Traffic accidents
119 General services (operator speaks Indonesian) or try Blue Bird Taxi, (Tel. 325–607) for radio-dispatched cars.

## Hours

Business offices are generally open either from 8:00 a.m. to 4:00 p.m. or 9:00 a.m. to 5:00 p.m. Official government office hours are from Monday to Thursday, 8:00 a.m. to 3:00 p.m.; Fridays, from 8:00 a.m. to 11:30 a.m.; and Saturdays, from 8:00 a.m. to 2:00 p.m. Post offices follow government

hours. Most foreign banks are open 8 a.m. to 12 noon Monday through Saturday. Local banks are open from 8 a.m. to 1 p.m. and from 2 p.m. to 4 p.m. English is widely spoken.

Shops are usually open from 9 a.m. to 5 or 6 p.m. Monday through Saturday. Tourist shops and the big department stores are often open until 8:00 p.m. Restaurants are usually open until about 11 p.m. Street stalls stay open later. Museums are often open on Sunday mornings, but are usually closed on Mondays. Go early to avoid crowds.

## Time Difference

There are three time zones in Indonesia. West Indonesia Standard Time, GMT plus 7 hours, covers the islands of Sumatra, Java, Madura and Bali; Central Indonesia Standard Time is GMT plus 8 hours for Kalimantan, Sulawesi and Nusa Tenggara; and East Indonesia Standard Time is GMT plus 9 hours for Maluku and Irian.

## Museums

**The National Museum,** founded more than two centuries ago, has one of the largest collections in Southeast Asia. It is divided into five main sections: Monumental Stones, Pre-history, Ethnography, Ceramics and The Treasure Room upstairs. The opening hours are bewildering so double check the following list before going: Sundays and Tuesdays through Thursdays from 8:30 a.m. 2:30 p.m.; Friday from 8:30 a.m. to 11 a.m.; and Saturday from 8:30 a.m. to 1:30 p.m. Always closed on Mondays.

**Museum Bahari** (Marine Museum), in the Sunda Kelapa harbor area, is located in the remains of a beautifully-restored Dutch warehouse from the first trading post of the Dutch East India Company in Java. Replicas of ships that ply the islands are on display. Don't miss the view of the area from atop the old Lookout Tower nearby. It is open daily from 9 a.m. to 2 p.m., Fridays until 11 a.m., Saturdays until 1 p.m. and Sundays until 3 p.m. Closed Mondays. Perfect for wistful wonderers.

There are three fine museums in the Taman Fatahillah Restoration District that operate during the same hours as Museum Bahari. The **Jakarta History Museum** in the Old Batavia City Hall depicts the historical development of Jakarta through displays of artifacts, furniture, portraits and household items from the homes of wealthy plantation owners. East of the square, **Bali Seni Rupa and Museum Keramik** (The Museum of Fine Arts and Ceramics) houses a valuable collection of ceramics and a permanent exhibition of Indonesia's master painters. At the west end of the square the **Wayang Museum** has a display of some of Indonesia's finest puppets. It closes at 2 p.m. on Sundays.

**The Textile Museum,** Jalan Satsuit Tubun No. 4, has an exhibit of more than 327 kinds of Indonesian textiles from throughout the archipelago, including exquisite batiks and weavings. It is open from 9 a.m. to 2 p.m. daily, until 11 a.m. on Fridays, 1 p.m. on Saturdays and is closed Mondays.

**The Armed Forces Museum** (Satria Mandala), Jalan Gatot Subroto, portrays the development of the Indonesian Armed Forces and its role in the struggle for independence. It has dioramas of strategic battles. Open daily, except Mondays, from 9 a.m. – 4 p.m.

**Museum Indonesia,** Taman Mini Indonesia, takes a creative approach to exhibit the diversity of the archipelago. Its distinctive Balinese architecture is highlighted by an intricately carved gate. Open daily 9 a.m. to 3 p.m.

## Tourist Information Offices

It is a good idea to visit one of these offices for the latest brochures on Jakarta and special events. There is a Jakarta Visitor Information Service at Soekarno-Hatta Airport, (Tel. 550–7088). Jakarta Information Centers are located in the Skyline Building, a.k.a. Jakarta Theater Building, ground floor, Tel. (364–093), and Oriental Building, Jalan M.H. Thamrin 51, (Tel. 332–0679). The Jakarta Tourism Board is on Jalan Jenderal Gatot Subroto, Simpang and Jalan K.H. Abdul Rokhim, Jakarta, (Tel. 510–738, 511–369, 511–073).

## Toilets

Most toilets in Jakarta, even in small restaurants, are of the Western pedestal variety, so you should have no problem negotiating them. It is wise, however, to carry your own supply of tissues.

## Indonesian Customs and Taboos

The Indonesians are very polite people. Handshaking is customary for both men and women upon introduction or greeting and smiling is a pleasantly contagious national characteristic. It is rude to point at other people with any finger. Use the thumb or gesture with the chin. To point one's toes is also considered offensive, particularly if the foot is used to point to objects on the ground. Indonesians rarely spank children but give them a stinging pinch instead. Light pinches are also given to children as a sign of pleasure.

As in other Muslim countries, the left hand is never used to give or receive things, especially food or money. It is used for personal sanitary functions and traditionally considered unclean. Strict Muslims in Jakarta also believe dogs are unclean and feel uncomfortable around them. Most Jakartans follow Islamic dietary laws that prohibit the eating of pork

and some also will not eat shellfish or frogs' legs. On the other hand, many Balinese eat pork, but do not eat beef. Many Indonesians also do not care for alcoholic beverages. During the fasting month of Ramadan, strict Muslims do not eat, drink or smoke from dawn until sunset.

*Jam karet*, literally "rubber time," means exactly what it says. Meeting times can be very flexible so if you are a punctual person be prepared to wait. There is an abiding concern about drafts and breezes, both natural or from electric fans and air-conditioning, out of fear of catching a cold or *masuk angin* (best translated as a kind of debilitating flu). Don't be surprised that the windows are kept closed on a sweltering hot bus.

When addressing an older man, use the title *Pak*. With a mature woman, use *Ibu*. Address a young, single lady as *Nona*. Avoid confrontation at all costs in any situation and always stay cool, even if the dry cleaners just mutilated your new silk dress. Strong shows of emotion must be avoided to maintain your self-respect. Stay calm and level-headed.

## Photography

Kodak and Fuji color films are widely available. Processing of Kodak Ektachrome slide film and color prints is very good and there are numerous one-hour processing shops around town. Kodachrome film is expensive and, when available, includes the cost of processing which takes about a month at the nearest overseas Kodak plant in Australia. There is a Kodak Film Service Center at Jalan Kwitang 10 near the Hyatt Hotel.

For better natural light pictures avoid the intense daylight that occurs from 10 a.m. until 3 p.m. A skylight will help reduce the bluish haze of the strong midday light. To compensate for the intense sunshine, try moving down one f-stop.

The heat and humidity can ruin your film and camera. Carry and store your equipment with silica gel packets to reduce moisture. Be careful not to leave equipment in the sun or a hot car. When leaving an air-conditioned hotel, wait a few minutes to permit defogging of the lenses.

## Food and Drink

Jakarta is the best place in Indonesia to sample the culinary diversity of the country. Popular foods include *gado-gado*, steamed vegetables covered in a rich peanut sauce; *martabak*, fried Indian pancake stuffed with meat, egg and vegetables; *mie (or bakmi)*, noodles; *mie goreng*, fried noodles; *nasi goreng*, fried rice; *nasi uduk*, rice cooked in coconut milk; *sate (satay)*, bits of marinated meat barbequed on a skewer; *bubur ayam*, porridge with chicken; *sambal*, spicy hot chilis or sauce; *gule*, meat in curry

sauce; and *krupuk*, crisp shrimp crackers which make a good cover to hide the mountain of food you have taken from a buffet table.

Popular Indonesian restaurants listed according to their cuisine specialties include:

**Central Java**
Ayam Goreng Mbok Berek (fried chicken), Jl. Panglima Polim Raya No. 105, Kebayoran Baru.
Bu Tjitro's (famous *gudeg*, very popular speciality of Yogyakarta), Jl. Cikajang 80, Blok Q2, Kebayoran Baru, (Tel. 713–202).
**Sundanese** (West Java)
Sari Kuring (fish), Jl. Batu Ceper No. 55A, (Tel. 341–542).
**East Javanese**/Madura
Pondok Jawa Timur (soto madura soup), Jl. Prapanca Raya. It's much more than soup.
**Padang** (West Sumatran)
Family Restaurant, Jl. Melawai IV, Blok M. For those that like the spice of life:
Sari Bundo, Jl. Juanda 27, (Tel. 358–343).
**North Sumatran**
Sinar Medah, Jl. H.A. Salim.
**Makassarese** (South Sulawesi)
Happy, Jl. Mangga Besar Raya 4C, (Tel. 632–144).
Angin Mamiri, Jl. K.H. Hasyim Ashari 49, Roxy, (Tel. 377–241).
**Menadonese** (North Sulawesi),
Tinoor Asli, Jl. Gongdangdia Lama 33A.
**Seafood**
Jun Njan, Jalan Batu Ceper 69, (Tel. 364–063).
Sanur (Chinese), Jl. Ir. H. Juanda III/No. 31
**Others**
Satay House Senayan (several locations), Jl Cokroaminoto 78, seafood at some outlets.
Mirasari, Jl. Pati Unus 13, Kebayoran Baru, (Tel. 771–621)
Tan Goei, Jl. Besuki 1, Menteng.
**Rijsttafel**
Don't miss the experience of eating a *rijsttafel*, a banquet event right on your own plate. Heaped atop a base of rice are curried meats, fish, eggs, vegetables cooked in savory curry sauces, pickled relishes and the famous Indonesian sambal (the hot stuff). Nuts and a variety of crispy items add texture. Try the *rijsttafel* at the Oasis Restaurant, 47 Jalan Raden Saleh, (Tel. 326–397, 327–818).
**Western Food**
Memories, Wisma Indocement, Jl. Jenderal Sudirman. Offers pleasant lunch or evening dining amidst a massive collection of Dutch antiques.
Green Pub, Jakarta Theater Building, (Tel. 359–332). Excellent Tex-Mexican food.
Art and Curio Restaurant. Dutch Colonial style with big servings. Jl. Kebon Binatang III/8A, Cikini, (Tel. 322–879). Antiques for sale.

George and Dragon Pub, Jl. Teluk Betung 32, (Tel. 345 625). English food. Excellent Indian restaurant attached called The Curry House.

Rugantino. Italian. Jalan Melawai Raya 28, Kebayoran Baru, (Tel. 714–727). There are numerous Japanese, Korean and Chinese restaurants.

**Food stalls**

Sarinah Jaya, Blok M, at basement level along side the supermarket. Safe bet. Melawai Plaza 3/F. Stalls patterned after those in Singapore. Bintang, Anker and San Miguel are the three locally brewed beers, all are very good. The Indonesians learned their brewing techniques from the Dutch.

## Hotels:

Jakarta offers everything — from deluxe five-star accommodation with chic lobbies and modern facilities to small traditional guest houses.

### Expensive

These deluxe hotels equal their counterparts anywhere in the world.

Jakarta Hilton International (609 rooms), Jl. Jenderal Gatot Subroto, P.O. Box 3315, Tel. 587–981, 583–051. Tlx: JKT 46345–46673–46698 HILTON JAKARTA.

Borobudur Inter-Continental (866 rooms), Jl. Lapangan Banteng Selatan, P.O. Box 329, Tel. 370–108. Tlx: 44150 BDO JKT.

Jakarta Mandarin (504 rooms) Jl. M.H. Thamrin, P.O. Box 3392, Tel. 321–307. Tlx: MANDAJKT 45755.

Sari Pacific Hotel (500 rooms), Jl. M.H. Thamrin 6, P.O. Box 3138, 323–707. Tlx: HTISARIIA 44514.

### Moderate

Hotel Indonesia (666 rooms), Jl. M.H. Thamrin, P.O. Box 54, Tel. 320–008. 322–008. Tlx: 44233 HIPAJKT, 46347 HIJKT.

Hyatt Aryaduta (250 rooms), Jl. Prapatan 44–46, P.O. Box 3287, Tel. 376–008. Tlx: 46200 HYATT JAKARTA

Kartika Chandra (200 rooms), Jl. Gatot Subroto, Jakarta. Tel. 510–808, 511–008. Tlx: 45843 KACHA IA, KACHA JKT.

President Hotel (354 rooms), Jl. M.H. Thamrin 59, Tel. 320–508. Tlx: 46724 PREHOIA.

Sahid Jaya Hotel (514 rooms), Jl. Jendral Sudirman 86, P.O. Box 41, Tel. 584–151. Tlx: 46331 SAHID JKT.

### Moderate to Inexpensive

Sabang Metropolitan (157 rooms), Jl. H.A. Salim 11, P.O. Box 2725, Tel. 354–031, 357–621. Tlx: 445555 SAGANGIA.

Wisata International (165 rooms), Jl. M.H. Thamrin, P.O. Box 2457, Tel. 320–308, 320–408. Tlx: 46787 WISATA IA.

Orchid Palace (85 rooms), Jl. Letjen S. Parman, Slipi, P.O. 2791, Tel. 593–115, 596–911. Tlx: 46631 OPHIA.

Transaera Hotel (50 rooms), Jl. Merdeka Timur 16, P.O. Box 3380, Tel. 351–373.

Kartika Plaza (331 rooms), Jl. M.H. Thamrin 10. P.O. 2081, Tel. 321–008. Tlx: 45843 KACHA IA, 46470 KACHA JKT.

Marco Polo (181 rooms), Jl. Teuku Cik Ditro 19, Tel. 326–679.

Garden Hotel, Jalan Kemang Raya, Kebayoran Baru, Tel. 799–5808.

Jayakarta Tower, Jl. Hayam Woruk 126, Tel. 624–408, 646–760.

### Cheap

Wisma Delima, Jl. Jaksa 5.

Borneo Hostel, Jl. Kebon Sirih Barat Dalam 35, Tel. 320–095.

Majapahit Hotel, Jl. Majapahit 27, Tel. 356–702.

Bali International (31 rooms), Jl. K.H. Wahid Hasyim 116. Tel. 325–056.

Srivijaya Hotel, Jl. Veteran 1, Tel. 370–409.

Wisma Indra, Jl. K.H.A. Salim, Tel. 377–432.

## Festivals and Holidays

Many of the holidays in Indonesia are Muslim religious observances, but as a reflection of Pancasila, the state philosophy, Christian, Buddhist and Hindu holidays are also observed. The dates of the Muslim holidays vary from year to year, usually falling about 10 days earlier each successive year. The start of Ramadan, the fasting month, depends on the sighting of the new moon. The fasting month ends with the Lebaran two-day holiday when many Jakartans visit their cities or villages of origin.

In the following list of Public Holidays, only approximate months are provided for those with variable dates. The Muslim holidays are marked with an asterisk.

**January 1 –** New Year's Day.

**March –** Nyepi (Day of Silence in Bali and Hindu holiday celebrated nationwide in the spirit of Pancasila. A celebration of the Balinese new year.)

**April –** Mi'raj Nabi Muhammad* (Celebration of the Ascension of the Prophet Muhammad.

**March to April –** Good Friday

**May 8 –** Ascension of Christ

**May 23 –** Waisak (Buddhist celebration of the Anniversary of the birth/death of Buddha).

**June to August –** Idul Fitri/Lebaran* (Two day holiday that marks the end of the fasting month of Ramadan)

**August** – Idul Adha* (Muslim Day of Sacrifice. Animals are sacrificed in the grounds of the mosque and the meat is distributed.)
**August 17** – National Independence Day (Independence was proclaimed on Aug. 17, 1945.)
**September** – Muslim New Year*.
**November** – Maulid Nabi Muhammad* (Celebrates the Birth of the Prophet Muhammad.)
**December 25** – Christmas Day.

The following are special memorial days in Jakarta but not official holidays:
**April 21** commemorates the birthday of the late Raden Ajeng Kartini, the pioneer of the emancipation of Indonesian women around the turn of the century. Ceremonies are often held by women's groups and in schools.
**May 20** Hari Kebangkitan Nasional, National Awakening Day, honors the establishment in 1908 of a socio-cultural organization in Jakarta called Boedi Oetomo (High Endeavor), the first truly nationalist organization. The birth of Boedi Oetomo marked the beginning of awareness among the different ethnic groups in Indonesia of the need for unity to achieve national independence.
**June 22** The Birthday of Jakarta.
**August 18** Hari Pancasila, or Pancasila Day, commemorates the establishment of the state's guiding philosophy.
**Oct. 28** Sumpah Pemuda (Youths' Oath) Day commemorates the All Indonesia Youth Congress

held in Batavia (Old Jakarta) in 1928. An historic resolution was made at this congress proclaiming the ideal of one country, one nation and one language.

**Places of Worship**
The principle of religious freedom is evident everywhere. Jakarta has numerous churches, mosques and temples.
All Saints Church (Anglican) Jl. Arif Rachman Hakim 5, (Tel. 345–508).
Kebayoran Baptist (American Southern) Jl. Tirtayasa Raya 1/ Blok Q, Kebayoran Baru, (Tel. 791–062).
Baptist Bible Fellowship Jl. MPR III Dalam 3, (Tel. 762–837).
Calvary Baptist Church Jl. Gunung Sahari VI/36, (Tel. 343–652).
St. Canisius Chapel (Catholic – Mass in English) Jl. Menteng Raya 64.
Cathedral (Catholic) Jl. Katedral Lapangan Banteng, (Tel. 367–746).
Charismatic Worship Service (Assembly of God) Hyatt Aryaduta Hotel Jl. Prapatan 44–45, (Tel. 376–008).
Gereja Emmanuel (Protestant) Jl. Medan Merdeka Timur, (Tel. 370–747).
Jakarta Community Church (Interdenominational) Effatha Church Jl. Iskandaryah II, (Tel. 772–325).
First Church of Christ (Christ. Scientist) Jl. Teuku Chik Ditiro 48 Menteng, (Tel. 351–962).
Gereja Theresia (Catholic) Jl. Gereja Theresia, (Tel. 344–262).
Johannes Church (Catholic) Jl. Melawaii III, Block B Keb. Baru, (Tel. 770–763).
The Church of Jesus Christ of Latter-day Saints Jl. Dr. Saharjo 317B.

**Electricity:**
Most hotels use 220 volts/50 cycles. Outlets for shaving equipment are often in both 220 and 110 voltage.

**Children:**
Indonesians react so positively to children that you will find traveling in Jakarta with your little ones a pleasure. Restaurant managers and waiters are very tolerant (and helpful) when children become over – rambunctious. Reliable babysitting services are available in the major hotels. Disposable diapers are difficult to find. (Look in the Hero Safeway or Gelael Supermarket chains for diapers, formula and baby food.) Young children usually like to nibble on satay, small pieces of marinated meat on a skewer. Boxed drinks of fruit juices and long-life milk are very handy and available everywhere.

# Index/Glossary

# Photo Credits

**Diane Graham Garth:** Endpaper, 10-11, 16-17, 74-75

**Emmo Italiaander:** 12-13

**John Paul Kay:** Frontispiece, 30-31, 35, 41, 53, 62, 63, 65, 67, 72, 78-79, 80, 84 (left), 85, (left), 85 (right), 86 (right), 88 (right), 91 (left), 91 (right), 92 (left), 92 (right), 94, 99 (left), 99 (right), 106 (left), 107

**R. Ian Lloyd:** Cover, 14, 15, 22-23, 23, 27, 33, 36, 38-39, 43, 58, 59, 60-61, 66, 71, 77, 90 (right), 100 (right), 100 (left), 102 (left), 104 (left), 106 (right), 112

**Leonard Lueras:** 20, 21, 34, 37, 40, 86 (left), 96, 108 (bottom)

**Kal Muller:** 6-7, 8-9, 18-19, 24, 24-25, 42-43, 56-57, 70-71, 76, 86 (bottom), 88 (left), 89 (left), 90 (left), 97 (right), 98 (left), 98 (right), 99 (bottom), 101 (right), 102 (right), 103 (left), 103 (right), 105 (left), 105 (right), 108 (top), 109

**Luca Invernizzi Tettoni:** 4-5, 28-29, 44-45, 69, 89 (right), 93 (right), 95 (left), 95 (right), 101 (left), 104 (right)

**Paul Zach:** 87 (right)

Archival pictures that appear on pages 46-47, 48, 49, 51 (left), 59 (right) and 64 are from the collection of Leo Haks. All maps are by Viscom Design Associates, Singapore.

*The breathtaking sight of Bugis sailing vessels docked at Sunda Kelapa is one of the highlights of a visit to the Indonesian capital.*